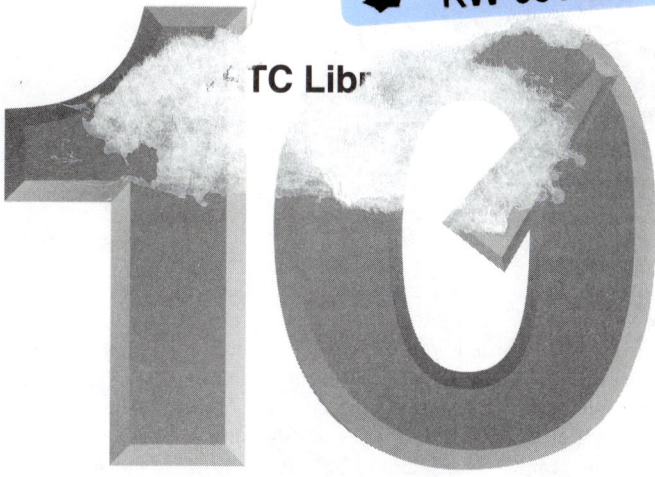

MINUTE
GUIDE TO
Lotus Organizer
2.0

by Robert Mullen
Revised by Jennifer Fulton

A Division of Macmillan Computer Publishing
A Prentice Hall Macmillan Company
201 West 103rd Street, Indianapolis, Indiana 46290 USA

To my mom, Cecile Label, to whom I'll always be the consummate beginner. —Robert Mullen

To my friend Jane, one of the most organized people I know. —Jennifer Fulton

©1995 Que® Corporation

International Standard Book Number:1-56761-580-5
Library of Congress Catalog Card Number: 94-079729

97 96   8 7 6 5 4

Interpretation of the printing code: the rightmost number of the first series of numbers is the year of the book's printing; the rightmost number of the second series of numbers is the number of the book's printing. For example, a printing code of 95-1 shows that the first printing of the book occurred in 1995.

Publisher: *Marie Butler-Knight*

Managing Editor: *Elizabeth Keaffaber*

Product Development Manager: *Faithe Wempen*

Acquisitions Manager: *Barry Pruett*

Development Editor: *Heather Stith*

Production Editor: *Kelly Oliver*

Manuscript Editor: *Audra Gable*

Book Designer: *Barbara Kordesh*

Indexer: *Brad Herriman*

Production Team: *Gary Adair, Dan Caparo, Brad Chinn, Kim Cofer, Dave Eason, Jennifer Eberhardt, Rob Falco, David Garratt, Erika Millen, Beth Rago, Bobbi Satterfield, Karen Walsh, Robert Wolf*

Special thanks to C. Herbert Feltner for ensuring the technical accuracy of this book.

Screen reproductions in this book were created by means of the program Collage Complete from Inner Media, Inc., Hollis, NH.

Printed in the United States of America

Contents

Introduction

It begins like this: your boss calls reminding you to attend an important meeting tomorrow. You frantically look around for the minutes to that last meeting with your boss, and suddenly realize the cleaning people must have taken them. They were in that cardboard box under your desk—you know, the one where you keep notes to yourself, records of phone conversations, and the minutes of important meetings. You begin to panic.

If that's not bad enough, the phone rings. A key vendor is calling you from the lobby to announce that he's here— right on time—and ready to meet with you. You don't remember making the appointment, but apparently you did. The vendor is here with critical materials, and the production lines will go down if someone doesn't meet with him immediately.

The day ends like this: your mom calls you at the office to apologize for forgetting your wedding anniversary. Oh no! What's the date today?! Where's that Post-It note that was supposed to remind you about your anniversary? Now you can't even go home!

It's time to get off the paper train. You need the *10 Minute Guide to Lotus Organizer 2.0.*

Why You Need This Book

Lotus Organizer is an electronic day planner, or *Personal Information Management* (PIM) application. Designed for use with Microsoft Windows, Lotus Organizer helps you keep your daily life organized.

This 10 Minute Guide teaches you *only* what you need to know in order to become productive with Lotus Organizer quickly, without a lot of technical details you don't want to

know or don't have time to learn. In short, concise lessons
that take less than ten minutes each, you can learn how to:

- Schedule appointments and meetings

- Keep track of special dates and events

- Make notes to yourself

- Manage a name and address list

- Keep track of phone calls you need to make or have
  made

- Print labels and pages suited for your loose-leaf
  organizer

- Create and maintain a To Do list

How This Book Is Organized

Each of the short lessons in this 10 Minute Guide include
step-by-step instructions for performing some specific task.
The following special icons also appear as a means of helping
you quickly identify particular types of information:

Timesaver Tip icons offer shortcuts and hints
for using the program efficiently.

Plain English icons define new terms.

Panic Button icons appear where new users
often run into trouble.

The following conventions have been used to clarify the steps you must perform:

On-screen text	Any text that appears on-screen is shown in **bold**.
What you select	Menus, commands, and options you need to select appear in color.
What you type	The information you type appears in bold and color.
Commands and Options	The names of menus, commands, buttons, and dialog boxes are shown with the first letter capitalized for easy recognition.
Key+Key Combinations	In many cases, you must press a two-key key combination in order to enter a command, for example, "Press Ctrl+X." In such cases, hold down the first key and press the second key.

Acknowledgments

Thanks to my wonderful teammates at Que for their contributions to this book: Marie Butler-Knight, Heather Stith, Kelly Oliver, Audra Gable, Herb Feltner, and our great production team.

Thanks also to Drew Berendts for his help with the Scheduler. I appreciate all the extra time he took to get it up and going on our office network.

Special thanks to my husband Scott, for understanding why I've been so busy lately.   —Jennifer Fulton

Trademarks

All terms mentioned in this book that are known to be or are suspected of being trademarks or service marks have been appropriately capitalized. Que cannot attest to the accuracy of this information. Use of a term in this book should not be regarded as affecting the validity of any trademark or service mark.

Lessons

Lesson

Starting and Exiting Organizer

In this lesson, you'll learn how to start and exit Lotus Organizer. You'll also learn about the parts of Organizer's screen.

Starting Lotus Organizer

Before you can start Lotus Organizer, you must have Windows running. If you haven't started Windows yet, do so now by typing WIN at the DOS prompt and pressing Enter.

> **What About Windows?** To learn some important Windows basics, check out the Windows Primer in the back of this book.

Once you've started Windows, you can start Lotus Organizer. Here's how:

1. Double-click on the Lotus Applications program group icon. The Lotus Applications group window opens (see Figure 1.1).

┌─Lotus Organizer icon

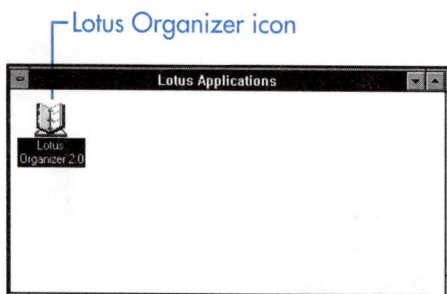

Figure 1.1 The Lotus Applications program group window.

Where's the Icon? If the Lotus Applications icon isn't displayed on-screen, you can access it from Program Manager's Window menu. Just click on the Window menu and then click on Lotus Applications.

2. Double-click on the Lotus Organizer 2.0 icon to start the program.

3. If necessary, type your password to log onto the network.

4. If you've already saved your work in a file, open it now. For more information on how to open an Organizer file, see Lesson 4. If you prefer, you can set up Organizer so that it automatically opens the same file for you each time you start the program; again, see Lesson 4.

Understanding the Parts of the Screen

Organizer's application window is made up of all of the usual Windows screen objects, such as the Control-menu box, title bar, Minimize/Maximize buttons, window borders, and menu bar. Other elements are unique to Organizer itself. Figure 1.2 shows the Organizer application window and the parts of its screen.

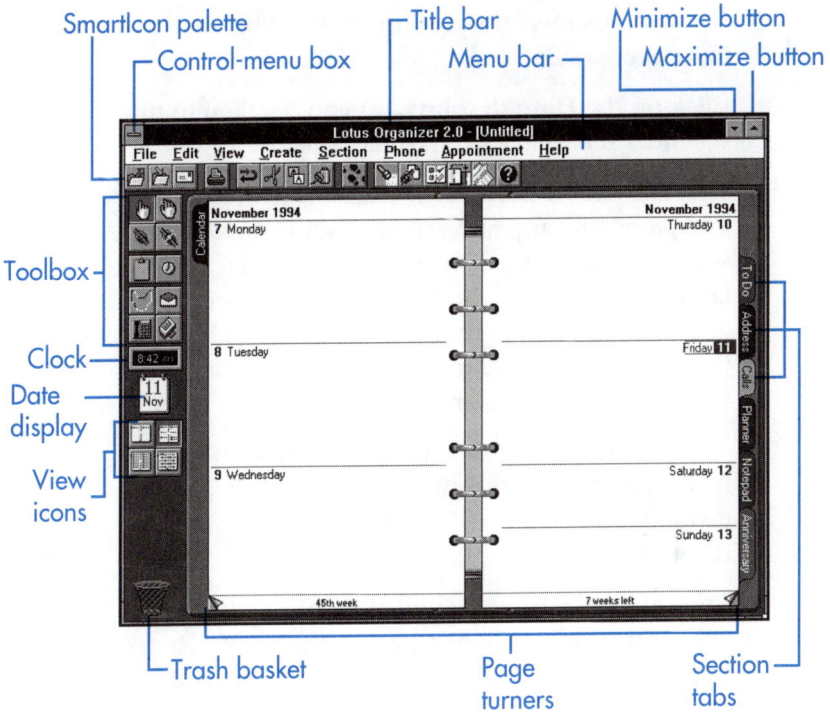

Figure 1.2 Organizer's screen.

Here are the main parts of Organizer's screen:

- The **SmartIcon palette** is a horizontal strip that contains a number of SmartIcons. You click on a SmartIcon to perform a common task, such as opening or saving a file. To see what a particular SmartIcon does, move the mouse pointer over the icon and read the bubble that appears. (Check out Lesson 2 for more on SmartIcons.)

- The **Toolbox** holds buttons that let you move entries, link information, turn to the previous page in the current section, send/receive mail, make phone calls, print information, and so on. To learn what a specific Toolbox button does, point to it and hold down the right mouse button.

- The **Clock** shows the time maintained by your computer system.

- Click on the **Date display** and you're taken to the Calendar section, open to today's date.

- The **View icon palette** includes up to four icons. The icons that appear vary depending on which section is currently displayed. To see what a particular icon does, move the mouse pointer over the icon and read the bubble that appears. (You must have the Bubble Help option on for this to work; see Lesson 3 for instructions.)

- You can drag information into the **Trash basket** from any of the six sections. When you drag-and-drop text into the Trash, it goes up in "flames" (it's deleted).

- The **section tabs** are found along the right or left side of the binder (depending on the view). Each of these section tabs represents a section, such as the Address or the Calendar. Click on a tab to switch to that tab's section.

- Click on the **page turners** to go back one page or forward to the next page.

About Organizer's Sections

Organizer is made up of seven sections. Each section performs a different task. If you use a daily planner now, you're probably familiar with these sections:

Calendar   Keeps track of important dates.

To Do list   Organizes what you need to do and when you need to do it.

Address   Records addresses and phone numbers.

Calls   Tracks information about calls you need to make or have made (such as their duration and status).

Planner Organizes events and related people.

Notepad Functions as an electronic pad of paper.

Anniversary Remembers important dates.

Organizer treats these sections as separate documents within a single file. Each single file is called an Organizer file. You can create and maintain as many Organizer files as your hard drive can handle, but you can only work with one file at a time. Most die-hard Organizer users keep two separate Organizer files: one for work and one for home. You'll learn how to create separate Organizer files in Lesson 4.

Quitting Lotus Organizer

To quit Lotus Organizer, follow these steps:

1. Open the File menu and select Exit Organizer.

2. If the file you've been working on has changed, a box appears asking you if you want to save the changes (see Figure 1.3). Click on Yes or press Enter to save your changes.

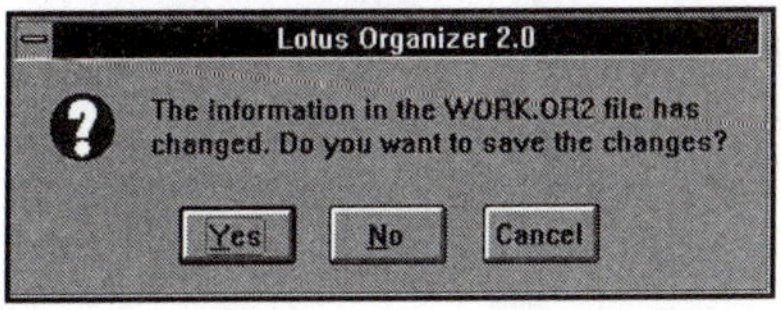

Figure 1.3 You may see this box when you exit Organizer.

3. If necessary, type a name for your file and click on OK. If you need more information on saving your file, see Lesson 4.

In this lesson, you learned how to start and exit Organizer. You also learned about the parts of Organizer's screen. In the next lesson, you'll learn about Organizer's SmartIcons.

Lesson

Using SmartIcons

In this lesson, you'll learn about Organizer's SmartIcons.

What Are SmartIcons?

SmartIcons act like push-buttons. When you click on a SmartIcon, Lotus Organizer carries out the task that button represents. For example, when you click on the Save SmartIcon, Organizer saves the currently active file. Because you don't have to use the menu system, SmartIcons minimize the steps needed to complete a common task.

Organizer is configured with several SmartIcons arranged together on its SmartIcon palette. Table 2.1 shows you those SmartIcons and their purposes.

Table 2.1 Organizer's SmartIcons

SmartIcon	Description
	Opens a previously saved file
	Saves the currently active file
	Sends an e-mail message
	Prints
	Undoes the last action
	Cuts data to the Clipboard
	Copies data to the Clipboard
	Pastes data from the Clipboard

SmartIcon	Description
	Backtracks to a previous page
	Searches for information
	Links files
	Shows through information from another section
	Includes a section
	Customizes a section
	Accesses Help

Customizing the SmartIcon Palette

Most of the popular SmartIcons are installed in the default palette, which is the one shown in Table 2.1. To customize the palette:

1. Open the File menu and select Organizer Preferences.

2. Select SmartIcons. The dialog box shown in Figure 2.1 appears.

Drag icons from here to the list on the right to add them to the palette.   ┌─Drag icons off this list to delete them from the palette.

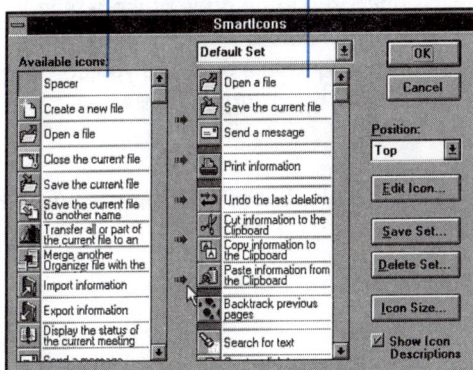

Figure 2.1 Customize the SmartIcon palette with this dialog box.

3. Drag icons from the list on the left onto the palette on the right to add them.

4. Drag icons off the palette on the right to delete them.

5. When you're through, click on OK.

Too Small?   If the SmartIcons are too small for you to see clearly, you can enlarge them. From the dialog box shown in Figure 2.1, click on Icon Size. Select a size and click OK. Then click OK again to return to the Organizer screen.

Moving the Palette Around the Work Area

You can change the way Organizer displays its palette of SmartIcons. You can position the palette along the top, bottom, left side, or right side of Organizer's screen. You can also make SmartIcons appear in an unattached, or floating, position.

Floating Palette   If the SmartIcon palette is *floating*, that means it is in its own window rather than being anchored to an edge of the screen. You can move the floating window around on-screen by dragging its title bar, and you can resize the window by dragging its borders.

To reposition the display of the SmartIcon palette, follow these steps:

1. Open the File menu and select Organizer Preferences.

2. Select SmartIcons. The dialog box shown in Figure 2.1 appears.

3. Select a palette position from the Position drop-down list.

4. Click on OK.

In this lesson, you learned about Organizer's SmartIcons and how to reposition and/or customize the SmartIcon palette. In the next lesson, you will learn how to get help from Organizer when you need it.

Lesson

3

Getting Help

In this lesson, you'll learn about using Organizer's Help system.

Using Organizer's Online Help

Organizer has a comprehensive Help system that can be accessed by simply pressing the F1 key (or by clicking on the Help SmartIcon) at any time. Lotus Organizer's Help is context-sensitive, which means that pressing F1 gives you a Help window for the task you are currently trying to accomplish.

> **Context-Sensitive** A kind of help that, when you ask for it, knows what you're doing and gives you very specific information. For example, if you press F1 while the Save As dialog box is on-screen, you get help information on saving files.
>
> Plain English

Lotus Organizer also has another type of help called *bubble help*. Bubble help works only with the SmartIcons unless you activate it. To do so, open the Help menu and select Bubble Help. Once bubble help is turned on, you can simply move the mouse pointer over an object of interest, and a bubble appears showing you help information. Bubble help is the fastest and easiest way to learn about something you see on your screen. Figure 3.1 shows the bubble help for the Print button in the Toolbox.

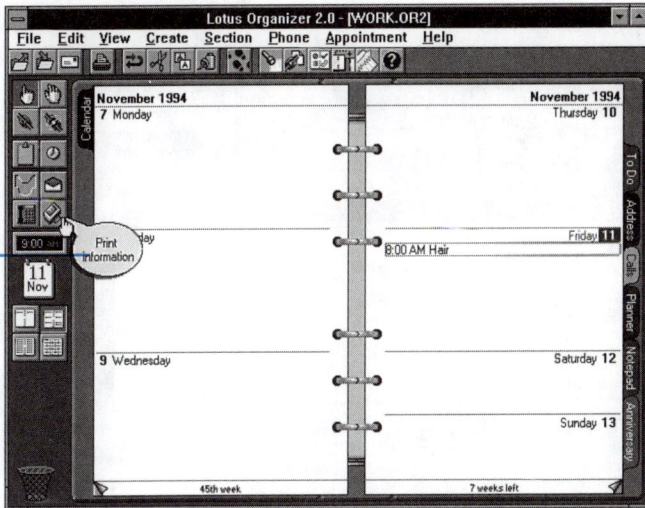

Bubble help

Figure 3.1   An example of bubble help.

The Help Menu

Although context-sensitive help is often handy, sometimes you might need help on a topic that is not related to what is currently on-screen. In that case, open the Help menu and select Contents.

From the Contents screen, click on any one of several categories. Doing so often provides you with a list from which to select more specific help. For example, when you select How do I? from the Contents screen, a Help window opens to show you a list of ten jump words that, when clicked upon, display Help text specific to that jump word (see Figure 3.2).

Control-
menu box   Details help   Click here to view
jump topic list.   Step by Step
help

Click here to see
Step by Step help.   Select a jump
topic from this list.   Click here to view
Details help.

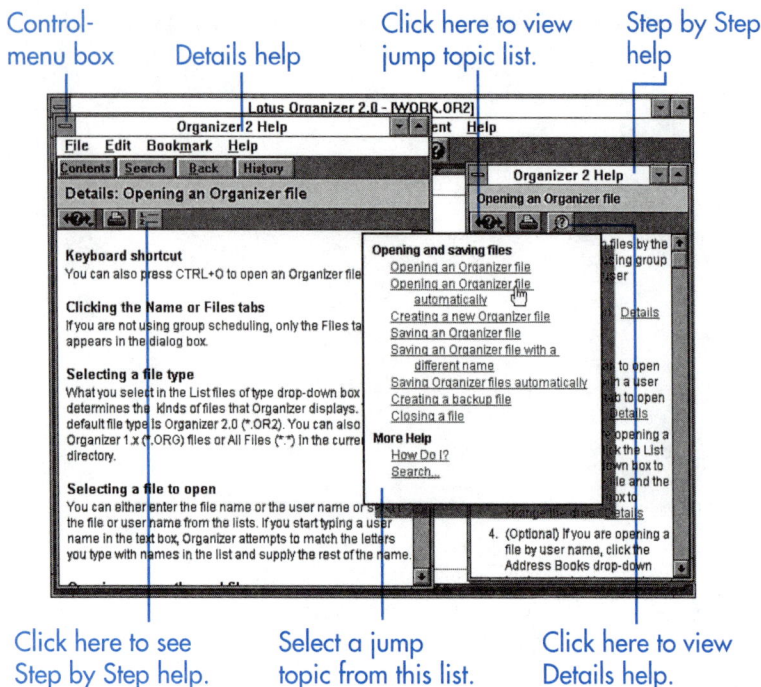

Figure 3.2   The Details and Step by Step help windows.

In the figure, I selected **Opening an Organizer file** from the Contents window. Another Help window (shown on the right in the figure) opened. This window displays step-by-step instructions for opening a file. Click on the question mark button to display the jump list again, and you can display a different topic in the Step by Step Help window. Click on the magnifying glass, and you'll see the Details Help window (shown on the left in the figure). Switch between these two windows as you like.

Jump Words   Words that you can click on to access more specific Help text. Jump words are usually indicated by the use of green text. Click on a green jump word to learn more about the topic represented by that jump word.

When you're finished using a Help window, double-click on the window's Control-menu box.

Searching for Help on a Specific Topic

The Search feature helps you find the most specific Help text related to a topic of your choosing. You can search for specific help by clicking on the Search button in a Help window or by selecting Search from the Help menu. Follow these steps to use the Search feature:

1. Click on the Search button, or open the Help menu and select Search. The Search dialog box opens, as shown in Figure 3.3.

Type a word here and press Enter...

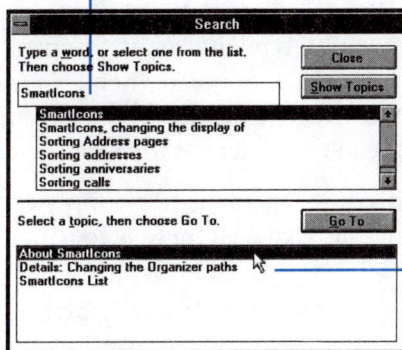

...then double-click on a topic.

Figure 3.3 The Search dialog box.

2. Type in the name of the item about which you want help and press Enter.

3. Double-click on one of the topics displayed in the lower box to go to that topic. Organizer displays Step by Step help on the topic of your choice.

In this lesson, you learned about Organizer's Help system. In the next lesson, you'll learn some basics about using Organizer files.

Lesson

Creating, Opening, and Saving Files

In this lesson, you'll learn how to create, open, close, and save Organizer files.

Creating a New Organizer File

When you first start Organizer, you have a new file on-screen that's ready for you to type in data. If you want to use any additional files, you have to create them. You might, for example, want to create separate Organizer files for home or work. You just can't use them at the same time.

To create a new Organizer file, simply choose New from the File menu. That's all there is to it!

Opening an Existing Organizer File

The first time you start Organizer, it opens to a blank notebook in which you can enter information. After entering the data, you save it in a file. From then on, when you start Organizer, you need to open this file in order to view or change its information.

Open Sesame If you use the same file each time you use Organizer, you can have Organizer open the file automatically each time the program starts. To set Organizer up for this, open the File menu and select Organizer Preferences. Select Organizer Setup. Type the drive,

directory, and file name in the Open file text box. For example, type **C:\ORG2\ORGFILES\WORK.ORG**. Then click on OK.

To open an existing file, follow these steps:

1. Choose Open from the File menu or click on the Open File SmartIcon. The Open dialog box appears (see Figure 4.1).

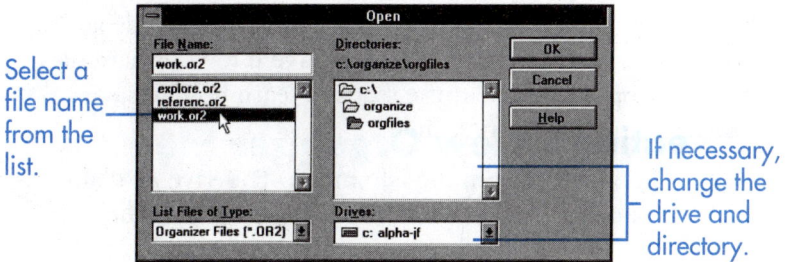

Select a file name from the list.

If necessary, change the drive and directory.

Figure 4.1   The Open dialog box.

2. If necessary, change to the drive and directory where the file is stored.

3. Select the file you want to open from those listed in the File Name list box and click on the OK button, or simply double-click on the file name. The dialog box closes, and your file opens.

> **Making the List**   To quickly open a file, open the File menu and check out the list at the bottom of the menu. Your most recently used files are listed there. Simply click on the name of the file you want to open.

Closing an Organizer File

Organizer won't work with more than one file open at a time. Therefore, you have to close a file in order to open a different file. If you need to save any changes to the open file, Organizer will prompt you to do so when you close it. To close a file, open the File menu and select Close.

Saving an Organizer File

Until you save your file, it is only stored in your computer's temporary memory (RAM). If you want to use the file again, you have to save it to disk. You can save it to your hard disk or to a floppy disk. Use these steps to learn how to save an Organizer file for the first time.

1. Choose Save from the File menu. The Save As dialog box opens. It looks like the one shown in Figure 4.2.

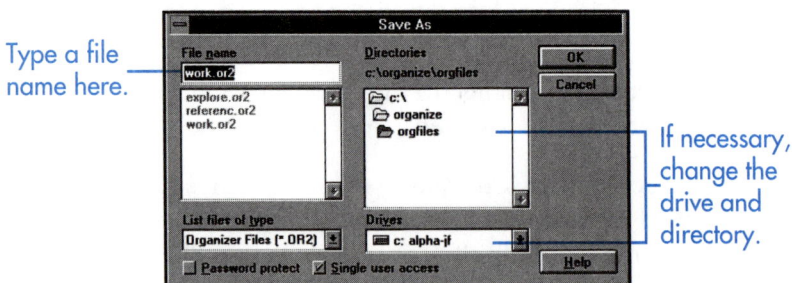

Type a file name here.

If necessary, change the drive and directory.

Figure 4.2   The Save As dialog box.

2. If necessary, change to the drive and directory where you want the file to be stored.

3. Type the name of your new file in the File name text box.

4. Click on OK.

Quick Save!   To quickly save a file, click on the File Save SmartIcon. The Save As dialog box will appear if this is the first time you've saved the file. Otherwise, Organizer simply resaves the file for you.

In this lesson, you learned how to create, save, open, and close Organizer files. In the next lesson, you'll learn how to navigate through the Calendar.

Lesson

5

Moving Around in the Calendar

In this lesson, you'll learn how to navigate the Calendar section of Organizer.

Looking at the Calendar

The Calendar works just like the calendar you have sitting on your desk or hanging on your wall. You simply turn to the page you want to look at and write down appointments and other things you don't want to forget. An advantage to using an electronic calendar is that you never have to cross off, white-out, or erase appointments that were rescheduled or cancelled. You can just move the appointment to a new date or time, or delete it altogether. (For information on changing appointments, turn to Lesson 6.)

If you've just started Organizer, the Calendar section is already open to today's date. To open the Calendar from another section, click on the Calendar tab. The Calendar opens to a page showing all the months of the current year. There will be a red square around today's date, as shown in Figure 5.1.

To open the Calendar to a certain date, simply double-click on the date. When you double-click on a date, the Calendar opens to that date's appointment page. If you want to go to a date in a different year, click on the appropriate year tab, and then double-click on the date you want. If you double-click on the name of a month, the Calendar will open to the appointment page for the first day of that month.

Year tabs

Year tabs

Click here to go directly to today's date.

Today's date has a box around it.

When positioned on a date, the mouse pointer is shaped like a hand.

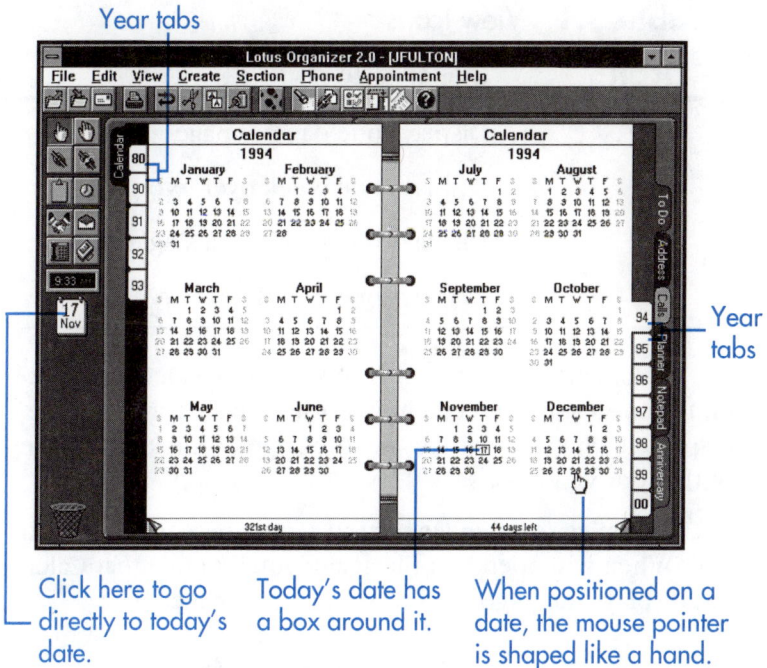

Figure 5.1   The first page of the Calendar shows the months of the current year.

Turn to Today   The fastest way to open the appointment page for today's date in the Calendar is to click on the Date display. (The Date display is below the Toolbox. It looks like a small calendar page.)

Changing the View of the Appointment Pages

When you're in the Calendar, there are four different ways (called *views*) that you can display the dates on the page. Each view is represented by an icon located beneath the Toolbox. The icons and their descriptions are shown in Table 5.1.

Table 5.1 View Icons

Icon	Description
	Displays one day per page
	Displays one week over two pages
	Displays one week on a single page
	Displays one month on two pages

Calendar's default view is to show one calendar week on two pages. If you need more or less space for each date displayed, change your view of the page by clicking on one of the four view icons.

Organizer's Calendar section remembers the view you like. When you open that file again, you'll notice that Calendar displays the page in the last view you selected.

Moving Through the Calendar

You can look into the near future or the recent past by flipping through the pages of your Calendar. When you're looking for a page just a few days away, you can use your mouse to quickly turn to it.

Look at the lower-outside edge of the pages of the Calendar. You'll see that each page looks like it's turned back a little. All you have to do is click on these lower-outside page corners to turn the page. Figure 5.2 shows these page corners.

If you want to turn to a page in a different month or a different year, click on the Calendar section tab again. You'll be returned to the first page of the current year's calendar, where you can select a new year or a new date.

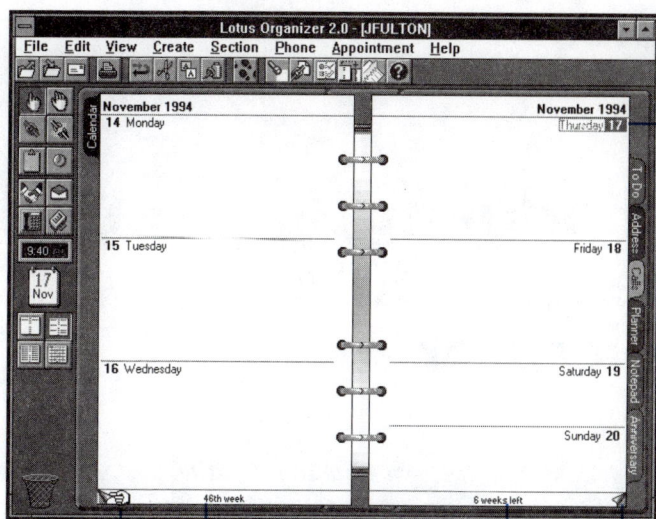

Today's date is marked in red.

The mouse pointer changes to a hand when positioned correctly.

The number of weeks until the end of the year is displayed at the bottom of the Calendar.

Turned back page corner

Figure 5.2 Turning to another page of the Calendar.

In this lesson, you learned how to move about within the Calendar. In the next lesson, you'll learn how to schedule and work with appointments.

Lesson

6

Scheduling Appoint-
ments with the
Calendar

*In this lesson, you'll learn how to schedule, edit, and delete
appointments in Organizer's Calendar section.*

Making an Appointment

If you work with people, you probably have to juggle com-
mitments and accommodate scheduling conflicts to get
together with them successfully. Lotus Organizer makes
scheduling new appointments easy.

To make new appointments with Organizer:

1. Click on the blank space under the day in which
you want to add a new appointment.

2. Double-click on the hour of your appointment. For
example, if your appointment starts at 1:00 PM,
double-click on 1:00 PM. If necessary, use the tiny
up and down arrows to scroll to the hour of your
appointment. The Create Appointment dialog box
appears, as shown in Figure 6.1.

3. Set the duration of the appointment in the Duration
spinner box by clicking on the plus or minus
buttons. This adjusts the duration in five-minute
increments.

Add a
description
for the
appointment.

Change the
duration, if
necessary.

Create Appointment

Date   Time   Duration   OK
11/17/94   10:30 AM   01h 00m   Cancel

Description
Jane Johnson   Add
Product Manager, CIS Systems
Discuss Redline project for January   Invite...

Find time

Categories Clients   Alarm...

☑ Warn of conflicts   Repeat...

☐ Pencil in   Cost...

☐ Confidential   Help

Set other
options.

Select a
category.

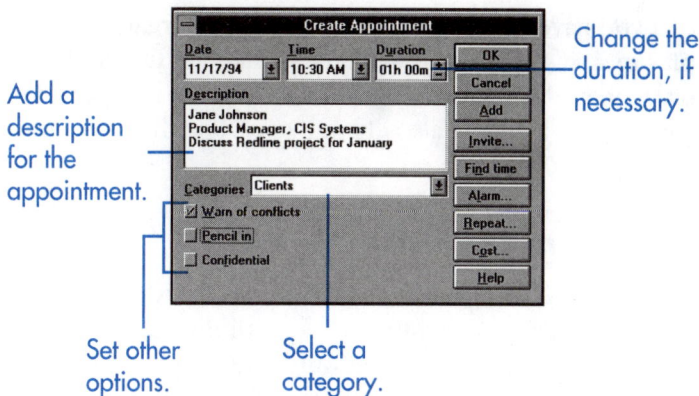

Figure 6.1   The appointment window.

4. In the Description area, type a description for your appointment. (This description appears on the appointment page. If the description is really long, you may have to scroll within the Calendar to see it.)

5. Select a category for your appointment from the Categories drop-down list. For example, select Clients.

6. Set the following options as necessary in each individual situation. Set the Warn of Conflicts option to have Organizer warn you of any scheduling conflicts; select Pencil In to set a tentative appointment (a pencil icon identifies a tentative appointment); select Confidential to prevent others from viewing this appointment if you share your file with them.

7. Click on OK to schedule the appointment.

Can I Repeat That?   If you want to repeat an appointment entry automatically, see Lesson 8. You can also add cost codes and set an alarm for this appointment, which you'll learn about in Lesson 8.

If you have too many appointments for Organizer to display in a single day's view, you can click on the down arrow icon at the bottom of the day's text area to see more appointments. You can also change to a view that gives more space to each day.

Dealing with Conflicts

If you try to add an appointment that conflicts with another appointment, Organizer notifies you with the dialog box shown in Figure 6.2. (Organizer only notifies you of conflicts with meetings if you select the Warn of Conflicts box. However, it will warn you of conflicts with other appointments, whether you select the Warn of Conflicts box or not.)

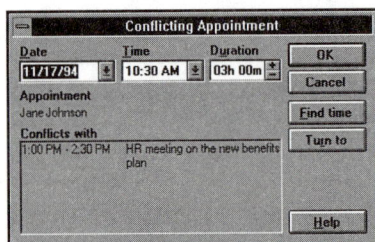

Figure 6.2 Organizer notifies you of conflicts.

At this point, you have several options. You can:

- Click on Cancel and change your new appointment so that it no longer causes a conflict.

- Click on OK and let the appointments conflict. (Conflicting appointments are displayed with a red line in front of them.)

- Click on Turn to, which adjusts the Calendar so that it displays the appointment page of the conflicting appointment.

- Click on Find time, which displays the first available time after the conflicting appointment. Click OK to reschedule the new appointment at that time.

Changing an Appointment

You can change appointment text at any time. You might, for example, want to change text about a meeting to compare the number of people who actually attended with those who accepted invitations. You also might reschedule an appointment, opting to leave the original appointment in place with an explanation for why you rescheduled.

Here's how you edit existing text in an appointment:

1. Double-click on the appointment you want to edit. The Edit Appointment dialog box appears.

2. Edit the text in the Description box.

3. Make additional changes as necessary. For example, you can change the duration of the appointment or add a cost code. If you need help adjusting the time or duration, see Lesson 7. If you need help adding alarms, cost codes, or repeating appointments, see Lesson 8.

4. Click on OK to save your changes and close the Edit Appointment dialog box.

Rescheduling an Appointment

Rescheduling an appointment is a snap! Follow these steps:

1. Navigate to the appointment you want to move.

2. Click on the Pick Up and Drop icon in the Toolbox. (See the Toolbox listing on the inside back cover if you need help.)

3. With the pointer, click on the appointment to be moved.

4. Turn to the day to which you want to move the appointment.

5. Click on a day to move the appointment to that day.

If you want to move an appointment to a day that's currently visible, you can skip the Pick Up and Drop tool, and simply use drag and drop. To drag and drop an appointment, click on the appointment and hold down the mouse button. Drag the appointment to its destination, and then release the mouse button to "drop" it.

Copying an Appointment

To copy an appointment, you follow almost the same steps as you would to move an appointment, but you use a different Toolbox icon.

1. Navigate to the appointment to want to copy.

2. Drag the appointment to be copied to the Clipboard icon on the Toolbox (see the listing on the inside back cover if you need help).

3. Turn to the day to which you want to copy the appointment.

4. Click on the Clipboard icon and drag it onto that day. The appointment is copied to the day you select.

If you want to copy an appointment to a day that's currently visible, you can use drag and drop. To copy an appointment, press and hold the Ctrl key. Then click on the appointment and hold down the mouse button. Drag the appointment to its destination and release the mouse button to copy it.

Deleting an Appointment

Sooner or later, one of your appointments will be cancelled and will not be rescheduled. With Calendar, it's easy to dispose of those pesky cancellations. All you have to do is drag and drop the defunct appointment into the trash.

Flames appear to show you that your entry has been deleted. Figure 6.3 shows the Trash basket icon and explains what it does (with a little help from Organizer's bubble help feature).

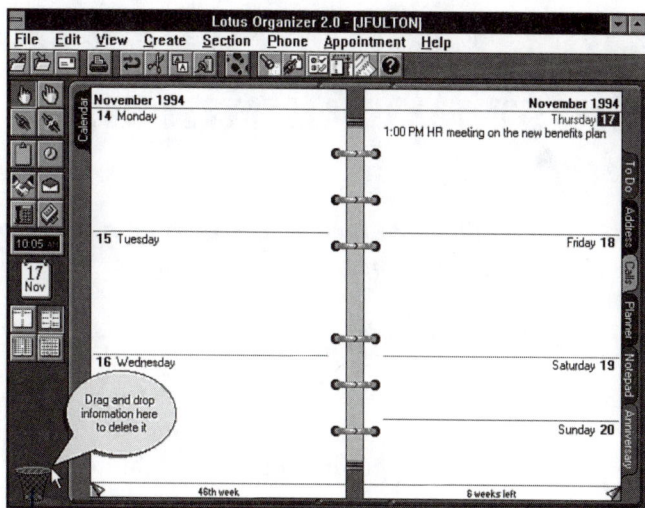

Trash basket
icon

Figure 6.3 The Trash.

> **Oops!**   You can retrieve a deleted appointment from the Trash basket by selecting Undo from the Edit menu or by clicking on the Undo SmartIcon. Act quickly, though: you can only save the last item you trashed!

In this lesson, you learned how to make and manage appointments. In the next lesson, you'll learn how to adjust the time and duration of an appointment with the time tracker.

Lesson

Using Time Tracker to Adjust Appointments

In this lesson, you'll learn how to use the time tracker to change the length and time of an appointment.

What Is the Time Tracker?

By default, the Calendar makes appointments for you that last 60 minutes. However, sometimes an hour isn't the right amount of time for the appointment. You might need to make more than one appointment in an hour, or you might need to allocate more than one hour for a weekly staff meeting or a seminar.

You can change the length and time of the appointment with the time tracker. The time tracker appears when you open the Time drop-down list box in the Create Appointment or Edit Appointment dialog box (see Figure 7.1). The time tracker consists of two clocks that show the starting and ending times for the appointment. The duration of the appointment is shown in a small box between the two clocks. You drag the elements of the time tracker up or down to adjust your appointment.

Drag the start clock to change the start time for the appointment.

Drag this to move the entire appointment to a different time segment.

Drag the end clock to change the ending time for the appointment.

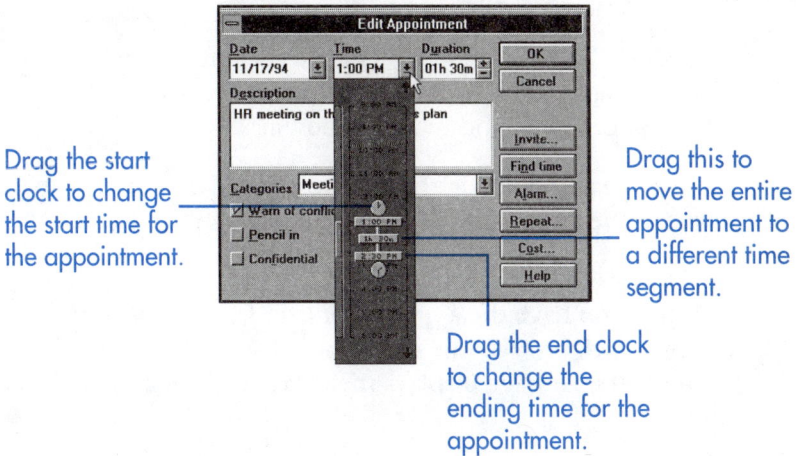

Figure 7.1 Focus on the time tracker.

Changing the Time or Duration of an Appointment

By default, the Calendar lets you choose only time slots that start on the hour or at half past the hour. However, you might have an appointment at 9:45 or 3:15. If that's the case, you can change the starting time with time tracker. It automatically adjusts starting and ending times by five-minute increments. Here's how to change the time or duration for an appointment:

1. From within the Create Appointment or Edit Appointment dialog box, click on the Time drop-down list box to display the time tracker. (To create an appointment, double-click on a day within the Calendar. To edit an appointment, double-click on it.)

Where's Time Tracker?   You can also display the time tracker by clicking on an existing appointment, and then clicking again.

2. Drag the upper clock to change the beginning time, or drag the lower clock to change the ending time for the appointment. The duration time will change as you drag the clocks up and down.

You can also click on the middle bar and drag to move the entire appointment to a different time slot.

3. When you have the appointment set for the correct time, click on OK. The dialog box disappears, and the Calendar page displays the correct appointment time.

Standard Duration   If you want to change the duration for all appointments, you can set the default duration time to a new number. For example, you can set the default to 30 minutes so your appointments are automatically scheduled to last half an hour. See Lesson 21 for more details on changing Calendar defaults.

Speedy Switch   If you want to move an appointment in 30-minute increments instead of 5-minute increments, hold down the Shift key as you drag the duration time displayed in the middle of time tracker.

In this lesson, you learned how to use time tracker to adjust appointments. In the next lesson, you'll learn how to set alarms, launch applications at specified times, and associate costs to appointments.

Lesson

8

Adding Extras to Your Appointments

In this lesson, you'll learn how to set alarms, launch an application at a preset time, and associate costs to appointments.

Setting Alarms

Calendar helps you remember important appointments by letting you set alarms. You can specify whether you want the alarm to be just a dialog box, or if you want the computer to play a sound as well.

Here's how you can set alarms for your appointments:

1. From the Create Appointment or Edit Appointment dialog box, click on the Alarm button. The Alarm dialog box appears, as shown in Figure 8.1.

> **Wired for Sound** Organizer uses the PC's speaker to make sounds. Make sure your computer's speaker is plugged in if you want to take advantage of Organizer's sound capability.

2. If necessary, change the number of minutes that you want the alarm to go off hours in advance of the appointment. (The default is 5 minutes.)

Change the number of minutes you want the
alarm to sound prior to your appointment.

Select a
tune or
display a
message if
you like.

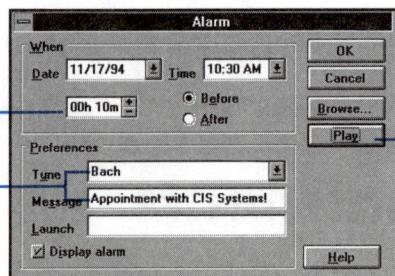

Sample a tune
by clicking
here once.

Figure 8.1 The Alarm dialog box.

3. Set these additional options, as necessary:

- If you want Organizer to play a tune when the
alarm goes off, choose one from the Tune list
box. To preview a tune, click on Play.

- If you want Organizer to display a message when
the alarm goes off, type it in the Message box.

4. Click on the OK button to return to the Create
Appointment or Edit Appointment dialog box.

If you have the Calendar set up to display the alarm
symbol, you'll see a bell displayed in front of the appointment. For help setting the Calendar up to do this, see
Lesson 21.

When your alarm goes off, a dialog box appears on your
screen. This alarm dialog box is displayed in the foreground
while you're using any Windows application. If you selected
a tune for the alarm, you'll hear the tune you chose and see a
dialog box that displays your appointment text. If necessary,
you can click on Snooze to be reminded again in another five
minutes. If you want more detail on the appointment, click
on Turn to, and you'll be taken to the entry in your Calendar.
Otherwise, simply click on OK.

IMPORTANT: Note that Organizer must be running in order for your alarms to go off at all.

Repeating Appointments

You can repeat an appointment automatically without re-entering it. For example, if you have a weekly meeting, you can enter it once and then repeat it by following these steps:

1. From the Create Appointment or Edit Appointment dialog box, click on the Repeat button. The Repeat dialog box appears, as shown in Figure 8.2.

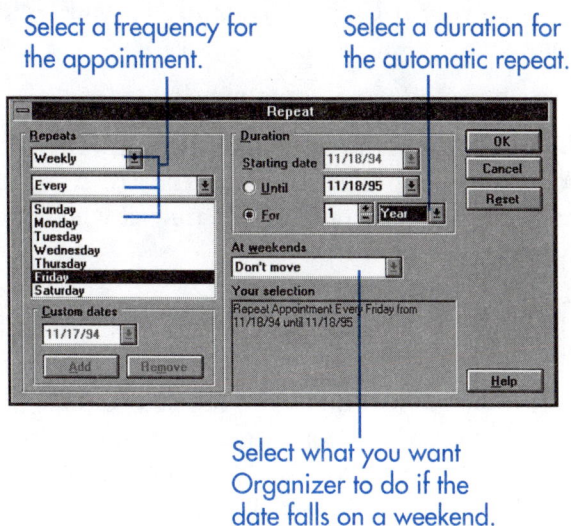

Select a frequency for the appointment.

Select a duration for the automatic repeat.

Select what you want Organizer to do if the date falls on a weekend.

Figure 8.2 The Repeat dialog box.

2. Select a repeat type, such as Weekly, from the Repeats list.

3. Select a frequency, such as Every Friday.

4. Select a Duration, such as 1 Year.

5. In the At weekends drop-down list, select what you want Organizer to do if a repeating date falls on a weekend.

6. Click on OK. You are returned to the Create Appointment or Edit Appointment dialog box.

Running Applications at a Preset Time

Just as you can set your VCR to record at a certain time when you're not home, you can set Organizer's Calendar to run applications while you're away from your desk. For example, you can set up your backup program to run while you're away from work.

Here's how you run a program using Calendar:

1. Double-click on the day on which you want to schedule your program to open the Create Appointment dialog box. Then, set the time at which you want the program to begin.

2. Click on the Alarm button. The Alarm dialog box appears (see Figure 8.3).

3. In the Launch text box, type the path and file name of the program you want to run. If you don't remember the exact path and file name, browse for it by clicking on the Browse button.

4. If you want Organizer to run the application automatically, don't display the Alarm box. Deselect it by clicking on the Display alarm check box.

5. Click on the OK button to return to the Create Appointment dialog box.

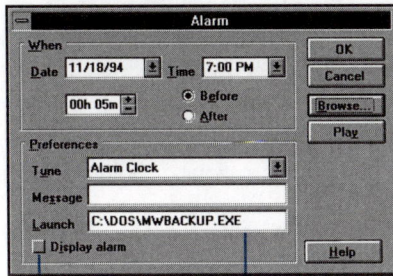

Turn this off if you want to run your application when you're not there.

Type the path and file name here.

Figure 8.3 Setting an alarm.

Didn't Work? Remember, Organizer has to be running (either minimized or full-screen) at the time the application is supposed to be launched.

Associating Costs to Specific Appointments

If you're one of those folks who has to track his time against projects, budgets, cost center codes, or customer purchase order numbers, you'll be interested in learning how to use Organizer's Calendar to attribute and track costs against appointments.

Here's how you assign a cost to an appointment:

1. Double-click on your appointment to open the Edit Appointment dialog box or create a new appointment.

2. Click on the Cost button, and the Cost dialog box appears, as shown in Figure 8.4.

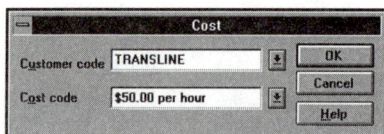

Figure 8.4   Add costs to your appointments.

3. Enter the customer code into the Customer code text box. The customer code can be as simple as the customer's name (such as a company name) or as systematic as a cost center number (probably provided by your company's accounting department). Once you enter a customer code, it is added to a permanent list from which you can choose later.

4. Enter the amount you charge per hour for your time in the Cost code text box. Once you enter a cost code, it is added to a permanent list from which you can choose later.

5. Click on the OK button when you're finished.

If you've set up the Calendar to display cost codes, your customer and cost codes appear under the appointment. See Lesson 21 for help with setting up the Calendar in this way.

In this lesson, you learned how to use Organizer's Calendar to set alarms, launch programs, and associate costs with appointments. In the next lesson, you'll learn how to use the Calendar to schedule meetings.

Lesson

9

Scheduling Meetings

In this lesson, you'll learn how to use the Calendar to schedule meetings with your associates.

Inviting Someone to a Meeting

If you are on a network, you can use the scheduling feature in Organizer to schedule meetings between yourself and several associates. You can even reserve meeting rooms and other equipment (such as a projector) with this feature.

> **What Meeting?**   Your network administrator must first install the Schedule Advisor for you to use this feature. Consult with your network administrator before you try to schedule meetings.

When you schedule a meeting yourself, you become the "chairperson," meaning that you control who's invited and what resources are scheduled for the meeting. When people respond to the meeting notice, you are automatically notified.

Here's how to schedule a meeting:

1. Set up the meeting just as you would any other appointment, by double-clicking on a day and completing the Create Appointment dialog box. (See Lesson 6 if you need help.)

2. From the Create Appointment dialog box, click on Invite. The Schedule Meeting dialog box appears (see Figure 9.1).

Times that are already
booked appear in blue.

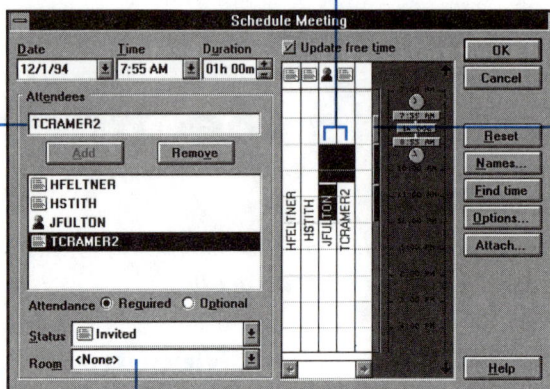

Type in a
name, or use
the Names
box to select
one.

Your meeting
time appears
in green
when there
are no
conflicts.

Select a meeting
room here.

Figure 9.1 By invitation only.

3. Select the people you would like to invite by typing
their names in the Attendees text box and clicking
on Add. If you prefer, you can click on the Names
button, select attendees from the list, and then click
on Add.

Select any necessary resources (such as a room or a
projector) from the Room list.

If there is a particular person who must attend, click
on the Required button after selecting his or her
name.

4. As you select attendees, their time-lines appear with
times that are already booked marked in blue. (If a
time-line doesn't appear, your attendee does not use
Organizer; however, he will still be notified of the
meeting via electronic mail.) Your meeting time
appears in green as long as there are no conflicts; if
there are conflicts, it appears in red. If necessary,
you can resolve conflicts in one of three ways:

- Drag the meeting bar to a new time slot.

- Change the date of the meeting.

- Click on the Find Time button, and Organizer finds the next available time slot. Click Reset if you don't like the time Organizer has picked.

5. When you're through, click on OK. Organizer sends a meeting notice to all attendees. As they respond, you are notified.

> **Meeting Minutes**   You can send along a copy of the proposed minutes (or any other file, for that matter) with your invitation. From the Schedule Meeting dialog box, click on the Attach button, enter the name of the file you want to send, and then click on OK.

You can change the meeting later on, just as you can any other appointment. If you change a meeting, all of the original invitees are notified of the change. If you delete a meeting by dragging it to the Trash basket, all invitees *who accepted* are notified.

Tracking Responses to Your Invitation

As the chairperson for the meeting you arranged, you are responsible for tracking the responses of your invitees. When a person receives an invitation to a meeting, they either accept, decline, or pass the invitation on to someone else. When the person responds, the hands of the Meeting Notice icon in the Toolbox start shaking. You can then check the status of responses by following these steps:

1. Click on the Meeting Notices icon in the Toolbox, or open the File menu and select Meeting Notices. The Meeting Notices dialog box appears.

2. Select a response from the list and click on Open. A dialog box appears. (See Figure 9.2.)

This person
delegated
MWATSON
to attend in
her place.

A check mark
means he has
accepted; an
"X" means he
has declined.

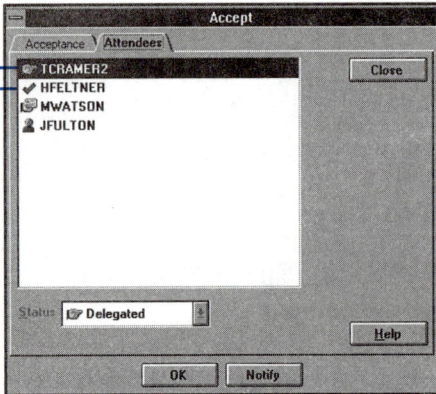

Figure 9.2 Check on the status of your meeting with this dialog box.

3. If the respondent sent a message, click on the Message tab to view it. (The Message tab does not appear unless the respondent sent you a message.) Otherwise, click on the Attendees tab to verify the status of all the attendees: a check mark indicates the person will attend, an "X" indicates that he will not attend, and an arrow indicates that your original person delegated a substitute.

4. To notify the attendee that you've received his message, click on Notify.

5. Click on Close to return to the Meeting Notice dialog box.

6. Click on Close again to return to Organizer.

Put It on Automatic You can automatically reply to the notices from your attendees by setting the appropriate options under File, Organizer Preferences, Meeting Notices.

Responding to an Invitation

When you're invited to a meeting yourself, the hands of the
Meeting Notice icon in the Toolbox start shaking. At that
time, you can view a description of the meeting and then
respond. Here's how:

1. Open the File menu and select Meeting Notices, or
   click on the Meeting Notices icon. The Meeting
   Notices dialog box appears.

2. Select a meeting and then click Open. The dialog
   box shown in Figure 9.3 appears.

Change the meeting
description here.

Check out who
else is attending.

Send a typed
message.

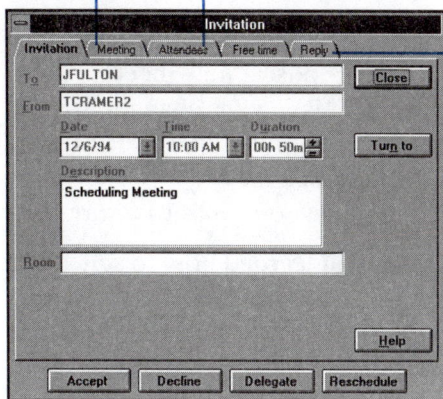

Figure 9.3 Responding to a meeting.

3. To see who's attending, click on the Attendees tab.

4. To type a reply, click on the Reply tab and type a
   message.

5. If you want, click on the Meeting tab and change
   the description of the meeting. You can also use
   this tab to "pencil in" a meeting instead of actually
   confirming it.

6. Check your own free time by clicking on the Free time tab. Then click on Accept or Decline. If you accept the invitation, it appears in your calendar with a shaking-hands icon.

7. Click on OK to return to the Meeting Notices dialog box. Because you've responded to it, the meeting is removed from the notices box.

8. Click on OK to return to Organizer.

You can delegate someone else to take your place by clicking on the Delegate button in step 6. Under To, type the name of the person you want to delegate. You can check his free time status by clicking on the Free time tab. Click on Send Delegation to send the notice. Then click on Close to return to Organizer.

If you want to propose a new meeting time, click on Reschedule in step 6. Make your changes to the meeting notice, and then click on the Free time tab to verify that everyone can attend. Click on Propose Reschedule to send the notice, and then click on Close to return to Organizer.

In this lesson, you learned how to schedule and respond to meetings. In the next lesson, you'll learn how to work with the To Do list.

Lesson

10

Working with the To Do List

In this lesson, you'll learn about adding, managing, and removing tasks in Organizer's To Do list.

What Is the To Do List?

Organizer's To Do list is a single-page list that's made to accept any number of tasks. You can use the To Do list to plan and track almost every task you embark upon, and you can transfer the information directly into your Calendar section so you don't have to re-enter the same text there. When you've completed a task, you can mark it as "done." (A completed task has a check mark in front of it to denote completion.) The To Do list even sorts its listing of tasks by priority.

The trick to managing an effective To Do list is to make sure you give yourself enough time to enter tasks and maintain their status. The sections in this lesson teach you how to do just that: how to add to, manage, and remove items from your To Do list.

Adding Tasks to the To Do List

Most of us have more things to do in our lives than we can remember, let alone keep track of their priority and their current status. With Organizer's To Do list, you can enter as many items or tasks as you can find the time to enter.

To add a task to your To Do list:

1. Click on the To Do section tab on the right side of the Organizer's binder.

2. Double-click anywhere on the To Do page to open the Create Task dialog box (shown in Figure 10.1).

Enter a description.

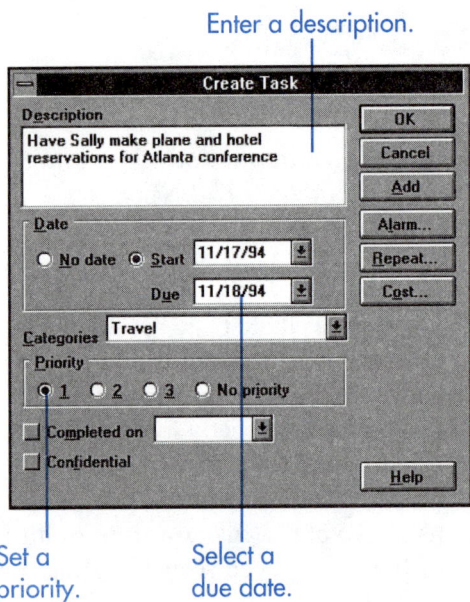

Set a priority.   Select a due date.

Figure 10.1 The Create Task dialog box.

3. Type the name of the task in the Description text box.

4. If you want, select a start date. Click on the Start down-arrow button to open the current month's calendar display. If you want, select another month by clicking on the left or right arrows, and then select a day of that month. Figure 10.2 shows you the Month display and the arrows you use to switch between months.

Click here to go to
the previous month.

Click here to go to
the next month.

| ◀ November 1994 ▶ |
Su Mo Tu We Th Fr Sa
30 31 1 2 3 4 5
 6 7 8 9 10 11 12
13 14 15 16 17 18 19
20 21 22 23 24 25 26
27 28 29 30 1

Currently
selected date

Figure 10.2   The Month display in the Create Task
dialog box.

5. Select a due date from the Due drop-down list in the
same way you selected a Start date.

6. If you want, select a category from the Categories
drop-down list.

7. In the Priority box, select a priority or click on No
priority.

8. If you consider the new task to be confidential,
click on the Confidential check box; otherwise,
leave it blank. If you use a Password, other people
will be limited by the security level you assign. (If
you want to know more about using passwords to
establish security, see Lesson 23.)

9. When you have all the settings the way you want
them, click on OK.

   Tasks are sorted by status (currently due, overdue,
future, and completed) and then by priority within that date.
You can change the sort order with the view icons located
under Organizer's Date display.

Managing Items

Once you've added items to your To Do list, you'll be ready
to manage them. You may want to change the date or the
priority, and you'll surely want to mark them as completed
once they're done. Here's how you manage the tasks on your
To Do list:

1. Open the To Do section.

2. Double-click on any task to open the Edit Task
   dialog box.

3. Select any of these options:

   - If you've completed the selected task, check the
     Completed check box, and a check mark
     appears next to the task in the To Do list. When
     you complete a task, the priority number
     doesn't change, it just goes to the bottom of the
     list. All completed tasks are sorted by date and
     then by priority.

   - If you want to assign the selected task to an-
     other date, use the Start and Due down arrow
     buttons to select other dates for your task.

   - If you want to change the order in which the
     selected task is slated to be completed, click on
     a different Priority option button.

4. Click on OK to save your changes on the To Do list.

What To Do?   You can view your To Do items
in other sections, such as the Calendar section.
See Lesson 21 for instructions.

You can repeat a To Do item automatically, without re-entering it. You can also set an alarm to remind you when an item is due. You can add both of these features to any item on the To Do list through the Create Task or Edit Task dialog box. Just follow the same steps shown in the Calendar section in Lesson 8.

You can control the information that appears for every item on the To Do list (such as categories, cost codes, and the color of overdue items). See Lesson 21 for tips.

Removing Items from the To Do List

Once you've completed a task, you can either leave it at the bottom of your To Do list (marked completed), or you can delete it altogether. It's entirely up to you. By default, Organizer's To Do list will not delete your completed tasks. You have to do it yourself.

To remove a task from your To Do list, follow these steps:

1. Open your To Do list.

2. Drag and drop the task into the Trash basket.

Deletion Anxiety   You can retrieve a deleted task by selecting Undo from the Edit menu or by clicking on the Undo SmartIcon. Remember: the Trash basket only holds one task, so you can only retrieve the last task you trashed!

In this lesson, you learned how to use the To Do list to create and manage tasks. In the next lesson, you'll learn how to add and manage addresses.

Lesson

11

Setting Up the Address Section

In this lesson, you'll learn how to set up the Address section; change address views; and add, change, and delete addresses.

Using the Address Section

Organizer's Address section is an electronic address book that can keep track of as many addresses as you want. Each bit of information about a single person is kept in its own respective field, based on what kind of information it is. All the fields for one address are organized into a single record for that person, and all records are organized into the database that forms your Address section.

> **Field**   A dedicated space in a database record. Specific types of information are stored in specific fields. For example, you store an address in a field used only for that type of information. Each record in a database holds fields that are found in every record.

> **Database**   A file or a group of related files that are designed to hold information. A database is basically a list with many columns of information.

Adding an Address

Adding an address to Organizer's Address section is easy.
Simply follow these steps:

1. Click on the Address section tab, and then double-click in the address area. The Create Address dialog box appears, as shown in Figure 11.1.

Enter business or home information
by clicking on these tabs.

Figure 11.1   The Create Address dialog box.

2. Click on either the Business tab or the Home tab.

3. Enter information in the fields that apply. Press the Tab key to move from field to field.

Back Up!   You can move backward through a record by pressing Shift+Tab.

4. Click OK to save the address. You can enter information under both categories (business and home)
in one step if you want. *Before you click on OK*,
simply switch to the other tab and enter the appropriate information.

> **Same Company?**   If you need to enter
> another contact for the same company, it's no
> problem. After you enter your contact's name and
> company, you'll see the Similar Address Found
> dialog box. Select the company from the list and click
> OK. The address and phone information are copied to
> the new contact's record for you.

If you want, you can change the field names to better fit
your needs. For example, you could name the two unused
fields in the Home section to include extra information (such
as the person's nickname). You can also change existing field
names. See Lesson 12 for details.

Viewing Your Addresses

Each address you add appears under the correct letter, as
shown in Figure 11.2. If a person has both a home and a
business entry, simply click on the appropriate tab to view
each one. The amount of information you see per entry
depends on the view. You can change between views using
the View icons.

> **Sorting Your Entries**   Your entries in the
> Address section are normally sorted by last
> name. You can sort your addresses instead by
> company name, category, or any other field, such
> as ZIP code. To change the sorting order, open the View
> menu and select Address Preferences. Select a sort order
> under Sort by, and then click on OK.

To view the home address, click on the tab. ⌐

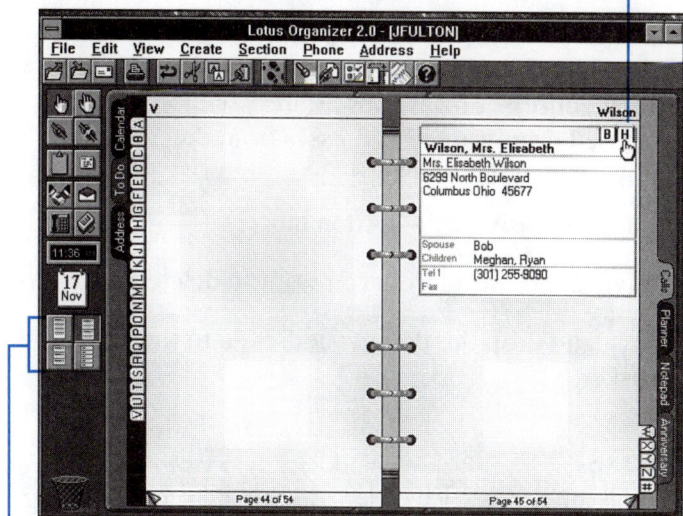

View icons

Figure 11.2 Viewing your addresses.

Changing an Address

Addresses often need to be updated. When a person moves or changes jobs, his address and phone numbers change. You can edit any address that needs updating by following these steps:

1. Go to the address you want to change by clicking on the Address section tab and clicking on the appropriate letter.

2. Double-click on the address you want to change. The Edit Address dialog box appears.

3. Make your changes and click on OK.

Deleting an Address

When people change jobs to the point that they are no longer a business contact, sometimes it makes sense to delete their addresses from your Address section. You can delete unused or unwanted addresses from the Address section by following these steps:

1. Click on the Address section tab.

2. Navigate to the address you want to delete.

3. Drag and drop the defunct address into the Trash basket.

> **Oops!**   If you delete an address by accident, you can undelete it by selecting Undo from the Edit menu or by clicking on the Undo SmartIcon. Don't forget to undo the deletion before you continue; you can only retrieve the last item you threw away!

In this lesson, you learned how to set up your Address section. In the next lesson, you'll learn more about working with the information in your Address section.

Lesson

12

Working in the Address Section

In this lesson, you'll learn how to find addresses, as well as how to customize address fields.

Finding an Address

If your Address section is bulging at the seams, it's probably getting harder and harder to find an address. Here's how you can quickly find addresses in your Address section:

1. Select Find from the Edit menu, or press Ctrl+F. The Find dialog box, shown in Figure 12.1, opens.

Type the name you want to search for here.

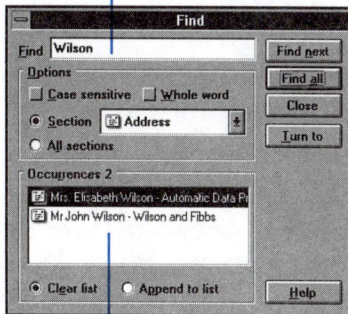

Figure 12.1 The Find dialog box.

Select a name from this list.

Search and Seizure   To quickly access the
Find dialog box, click on the Find SmartIcon (it
looks like a flashlight).

2. In the Find text box, type the information for which
you want to search. You can search for anything: a
name, an address, or a city. For example, if you type
Wilson, you might find entries for Elisabeth Wilson,
Wilson Street, Wilson, Pennsylvania, or Wilson
Industries—any entry that contains the word
"Wilson."

3. From the Section drop-down list box, select
Address. Now you're ready to search. (In Figure
12.1, I'm telling Organizer to search for the word
Wilson in the Address section.)

4. Click on the Find all button. Organizer displays all
addresses in which it finds your search text in the
Occurrences box.

5. In the Occurrences list box, double-click on the
address you're looking for (there may be more than
one entry listed). Organizer turns to the page with
that address.

6. Click on the Close button to remove the Find dialog
box from the screen.

Can't Find Your Address?   Be careful when
entering a name as search text. To search for
Mrs. Beth Wilson, you need to type **Wilson, Mrs.
Beth**, if that's how it appears. The more text you
type, the more specific your search will be (and the
greater the possibility of error). Therefore, it might be
easier to simply type **Wilson** or **Beth**.

The Address section should now be opened to the address you seek. If you're not looking at the right address, open the Find dialog box again and search for text you know is in the record. You can search for text in any address record as many times as you like.

Changing Address Field Names

When entering your addresses, you may decide to use a field for data other than that for which it was designed. For example, you may want to use the Assistant field under the Business tab for the spouse's name or a nickname. In addition, you might want to use the two unused fields under the Home tab and assign a descriptive label to them.

To change a field name:

1. Open the View menu and select Address Preferences. The Address Preferences dialog box appears.

2. Click on the Fields button. The Field Labels dialog box appears (see Figure 12.2).

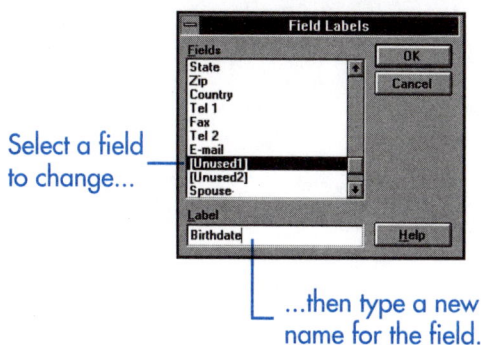

Select a field to change...

...then type a new name for the field.

Figure 12.2 The Field Labels dialog box.

3. Under the Fields list, click on the field you want to change. If necessary, scroll down until you can see the field you want.

4. Drag over the label, or press Backspace to erase the old label. Then type a new label.

5. Click on OK to return to the Address Preferences dialog box.

6. Click on OK again to return to Organizer's Address section. The field appears with its new name.

In this lesson, you learned how to work with your Address section. In the next lesson, you'll learn how to import and export address information.

Lesson 13

Importing and Exporting Addresses

In this lesson, you'll learn about importing information from other sources. You'll also learn about exporting addresses to other file formats.

Importing Addresses

Personal Information Managers, database programs, and even word processors can be used to keep lists of addresses. You can copy those addresses into Organizer's Address section. Organizer accepts addresses from dBASE III/IV, Excel, FoxPro, Lotus 1-2-3, and ASCII text files (such as Windows Notepad's format).

As you learned in an earlier lesson, databases (like Organizer's Address section) keep information in *fields*. If you're a spreadsheet user, it might help you to think of database fields as a spreadsheet's column or row labels.

You have to match up the fields in the imported database with fields in your Address database. You can have Organizer place information from the first field of your import file into the first field of your Organizer file (and so on), or you can link each field in the import file with a specific field in the Organizer file (this is more difficult, but safer).

Test Drive   I suggest that you try the importing process with the sample files located in \ORGANIZE\ORGFILES instead of your own Organizer file. When you're comfortable with the process, go ahead and use your own Organizer file. I'm going to use sample files from that subdirectory to illustrate examples.

Apples-to-Apples   The addresses stored in some ASCII text files need to be in a certain format in order for you to import them. Each field of information needs to be enclosed in quotes and separated from other fields with commas. All fields in one record need to be on the same line. You must end each record with a carriage return (the text editor you use may not display a carriage return symbol).

Here's how you import address lists created by other applications:

1. Open your Organizer file.

2. Select Import from the File menu. The Import dialog box opens, as shown in Figure 13.1.

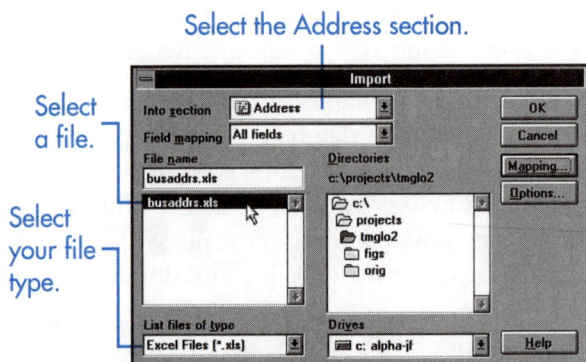

Select the Address section.

Select a file.

Select your file type.

Figure 13.1   The Import dialog box.

3. From the Into section list box, select Address.

4. From the List files of type list box, select the type of file that you're importing (for example, *.XLS for an Excel worksheet file).

5. If necessary, change to the drive and the directory where the imported file resides.

6. Select the file that you want to import (for example, BUSADDRS.XLS).

7. Click on Mapping. The Import Mapping dialog box opens, as shown in Figure 13.2.

Mapping   "Connecting" the data in the import file to different fields in Organizer. These connections tell Organizer where to place the imported information.

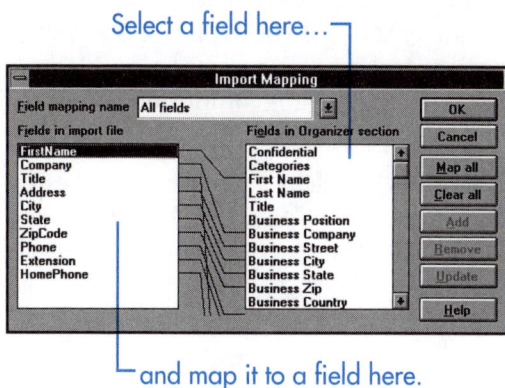

Plain English

Select a field here...

and map it to a field here.

Figure 13.2   The Import Mapping dialog box.

8. Use the dialog box to tell Organizer the fields in your Address section into which you want to place the imported information. Click on the Clear All button to clear the current mapping, which just maps the first field in the import file with the first field in your Address section, and so on.

Save Time! If you're importing another Organizer file, you can just click on the Map all button and skip steps 7–9.

9. To map each field, first select an Address field in the right-hand column, such as **Business Company**. Click on the Company field in the import file list on the left. See the line that connects these two fields? The two fields are now mapped.

10. Repeat step 9 until all of the fields in the import file are mapped.

11. Click on OK to close the Import Mapping dialog box and return to the Import dialog box.

12. Click on OK to import the data in the import file into the Address section of your Organizer file.

During the import process, you'll see a progress bar. In addition, Organizer will tell you which records can't be imported (usually because of formatting problems) and how many records were successfully imported.

Duplicating Work! If the same record exists in both the imported file and the Address section of the database section prior to importing, you'll end up with duplicate records in your Address database after you import.

Exporting Addresses

A database or word processing application can access the addresses in your Organizer Address database. You need to export the records in your Address section into another file format supported by Organizer. Organizer will copy your

Address records into a file that can be used by dBASE III/IV, Excel, Lotus 1-2-3, or any word processor that can read an ASCII text file.

When Organizer exports information, it organizes it so that these other applications can accept and utilize it. This process is called *field mapping*. See the "Importing Addresses" section in this lesson for more on field mapping.

Here's how you export addresses from Organizer's Address section:

1. Open your Organizer file.

2. Select Export from the File menu. The Export dialog box opens, as shown in Figure 13.3.

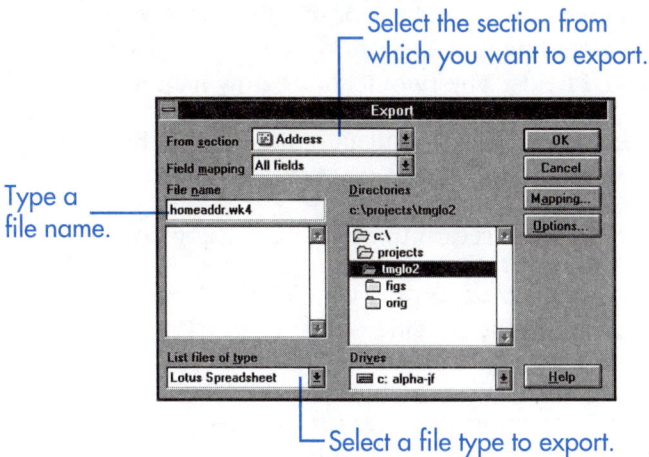

Figure 13.3 callouts:
- Select the section from which you want to export.
- Type a file name.
- Select a file type to export.

Figure 13.3 The Export dialog box.

3. In the From section list box, select Address.

4. In the File name text box, type a name for your export file.

5. If necessary, change to the drive and directory that contains the information you want to export.

6. From the List files of type list box, select the type of file you want to export.

7. Click on the Mapping button. The Export Mapping dialog box opens. You'll use this dialog box to tell Organizer which fields you want to place information in your export file.

8. If you don't want to export all the fields from the Organizer address section, click on Clear All. Otherwise, from the Fields in Organizer section list box, select a field to export.

If you want to export all the fields, simply click on OK and skip to step 12.

9. Click on Field 1 in the export-file field list box. Notice the line that appears between these two selected fields? The two fields are now mapped.

10. Repeat steps 8 and 9 until all of the fields in both lists are mapped to each other.

11. Click on OK to return to the Export dialog box.

12. Click on OK to export the data in your address database into the specified export file.

In this lesson, you learned how to use Organizer's Address section to import and export information. In the next lesson, you'll learn how to log and track phone numbers.

Lesson

14

Logging and Tracking Phone Calls

In this lesson, you'll learn how to log incoming calls and follow-up calls.

Logging an Incoming Call

With Organizer, you can track your incoming and your outgoing calls. All you have to do is tell Organizer about the call in progress and the outcome of that call.

To log an incoming call (you'll learn how to log outgoing calls in Lesson 15):

1. Double-click on a page in the Calls section, or select Phone, Incoming Call. Organizer starts its stopwatch and displays the Create Call dialog box, as shown in Figure 14.1.

2. Select a name from the drop-down list, and a company and phone number will appear. You can enter this information manually if the caller is not in your Address section.

3. Enter whatever Notes you'd like to keep. You must type some kind of note (perhaps a description) in order to save the call.

4. Change the Status of the call if you want.

Select the caller from your
list or type in a new name.

Add your
notes.

Log the
call status.

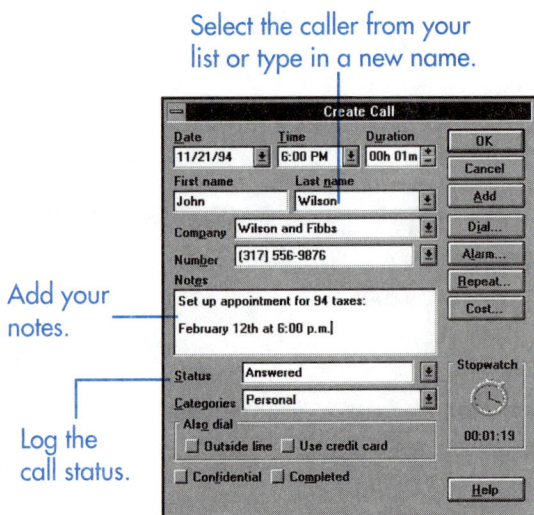

Figure 14.1   The Create Call dialog box.

5. In the Categories drop-down list, add a category for the call.

6. To enter a cost associated with this call, click on Cost. Enter a customer and cost code in the dialog box that appears, and then click on OK.

7. When you're done with the call, click on OK. The call is logged into the Calls section of Organizer.

> **Into the Future**   You can use the Create Call dialog box to plan future calls. Simply log the person you want to call and make a note as to the reason. To set an alarm to remind you to make the call, click on the Alarm button and set the number of minutes that you want the alarm to go off in advance of the call. You can select a tune to play or enter a message to display. Click on OK to set the alarm.

Viewing Your Calls

Once you have made or answered a few calls, you can view them in several ways within the Calls section. By default, calls are displayed in company name order. You can have Organizer display your calls by last name, company name, date, or category by selecting the appropriate View icon, as shown in Figure 14.2.

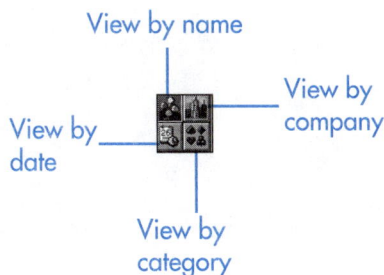

Figure 14.2   Use the View icons to change the order of your logged calls.

Entering a Follow Up to a Call

If your call is a follow-up to a previous call you've made or received, you can log it as such and keep your notes together. Here's what you need to do to log a follow-up:

1. Select the original call.

2. Open the Call menu and select Follow Up. The Insert Follow Up Call dialog box appears (it looks just like the Create Call dialog box), filled with the information about the original call. Organizer sets the Status automatically to Follow Up.

3. Add comments in the Notes section and make other changes as necessary.

4. Click on OK to log the call.

In this lesson, you learned how to log incoming calls, how to change the order in which you view your logged calls, and how to log a follow-up. In the next lesson, you'll learn how to log outgoing calls, and even how to set up Organizer to automatically dial a phone number for you.

15

Using the Dialer

In this lesson, you'll learn how to log outgoing calls. And if you have a modem, you'll learn how to get Organizer to automatically dial the phone for you, using phone numbers in your Address section.

What Is the Dialer?

If your PC is equipped with a modem, you can have Organizer dial the phone automatically for you using a program it calls the Dialer. After the call is dialed, the Dialer can release the line so you can talk on the phone. If your PC doesn't have a modem, you can still log your outgoing calls by following the steps in the "Having Dialer Make Your Calls" section. (If your PC has a modem but you don't want Dialer to use it to automatically dial your calls, simply set Dialer to the wrong COM port using the steps in the next section.)

> **How Does This Work Again?** If you want Dialer to automatically dial the phone for you based on a phone number you select, you need to connect your modem and phone correctly. Run a phone line from the wall to your modem. Then run another phone line from the phone connector in your modem to your phone.

Setting Up Dialer

To enable Organizer to dial the phone for you, you must first set up the Dialer program:

1. Open the File menu and select Organizer Preferences.

2. Select Dialer. The Dialer Preferences dialog box appears, as shown in Figure 15.1.

Change the COM port to match your modem's.

Check here to use your phone for all calls you make with Organizer.

Add calling card numbers here.

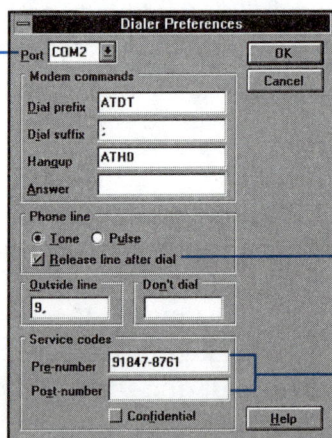

Figure 15.1 The Dialer Preferences dialog box.

3. Change the Port (connection port) to match the setting for your modem, if necessary.

4. To have Organizer release the line to your telephone after your call has been dialed, click on Release line after dial.

Hi, It's My Computer Calling   If you don't select the Release line after dial option, you should only use Dialer to call other computers. Otherwise, when you pick up your phone the modem will hang onto the line, and you won't hear anything.

5. Under Outside line, type the numbers you want Organizer to dial in order to get a dial tone. (By default, Organizer is set up to dial a "9" to get an outside line.) If you don't need to dial anything to get an outside line, delete the 9 and the comma.

6. Under Service codes, enter a number or code (such as a credit card number or access code) that you want Organizer to dial either before or after it dials your number.

7. Click on OK to save your Dialer information.

No Dial Tone?   If you don't get a dial tone when using the Dialer, first verify that the phone line is active and that it's connected to the modem (and from the modem to the phone) correctly. Next, try changing the Port setting and then try again.

Having Dialer Make Your Call

Once you have Dialer set up, you can use it to dial any number for you by following these steps. (If you disabled the modem or if your PC does not have a modem, you can still follow these steps to log an outgoing call.)

1. Click on the Phone icon on Organizer's toolbox. (It looks like a small telephone.) The Dial dialog box appears (see Figure 15.2).

70

Lesson 15

Select the person to dial.

Click here if you
need Organizer
to get you an
outside line.

Click here to use
your calling card
number.

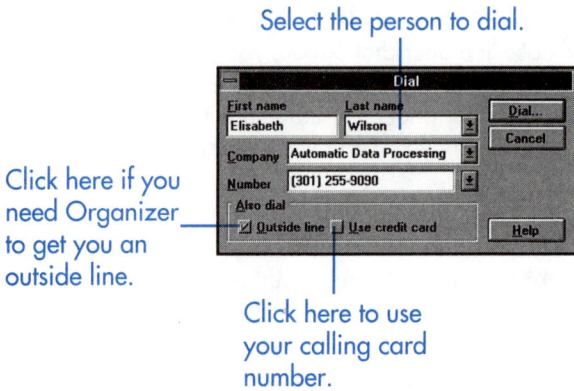

Figure 15.2 The Dial dialog box.

Autodial Shortcut While using the Address
section, you can automatically dial someone by
dragging-and-dropping an address (or any other
entry that contains a phone number) onto the
Phone icon in the Toolbox.

2. Select a name from the drop-down list box or type
the number you want to dial.

3. Click on the Outside line check box to use the code
you entered in the Dialer Preferences dialog box to
gain access to an outside line.

4. If you want to use the calling card information you
entered in the Dialer Preferences dialog box, click
on Use credit card.

5. Click on the Dial button. Your modem dials the
phone for you.

6. When it connects, pick up the phone and begin talking. The modem will release the line (providing you selected that option in the Dialer Preferences dialog box).

7. When the Dialing dialog box opens, log your call by clicking on the button under Log call as that best describes the outcome of your call. The Create Call dialog box opens, and you can make notes.

8. Click on OK when you finish making your call. Dialer will note the length of the call and add that to your description.

A Hang Up   Some modems have a hard time hanging up when you ask them to. If your modem fails to hang up properly when you click on the Hang up button, click on the Phone icon again, but this time type **++ATH** instead of a phone number. Dialing this character sequence forces most Hayes-compatible modems to hang up. If the modem still doesn't hang up, click on the Retry button in the Dialing dialog box until you regain your dial tone.

In this lesson, you learned how to set up Organizer to dial phone numbers for you automatically and how to log manually-dialed outgoing calls. In the next lesson, you'll learn how to work with Organizer's planner section.

16

Working with the Planner

In this lesson, you'll learn how to change your view of the Planner, add events, use the Calendar in conjunction with the Planner, and work with resources, such as meeting rooms.

What Is the Planner?

Organizer's Planner (shown in Figure 16.1) is intended to resemble a chart that you can update continuously. You use the Planner to allocate blocks of time for events. The Planner includes a separate chart for each year (through 2000). When you open the Planner, the current year's chart is displayed across two pages. You can reduce the chart to a single page by clicking on the Fold Page icon.

Planner's charts show you colored blocks that represent planned events over the course of the year. Months are listed from top-to-bottom. The days in each month are displayed along the top of the chart from left-to-right. Since months vary (in the number of Sundays, for example), you may see a month's schedule begin on the second or even the third day of the week. The beginning of a month is marked with a red triangle icon. Weekends are grayed-out so that you can distinguish them easily.

Drag the cursor over
dates to create an event.

Fold Page
icon

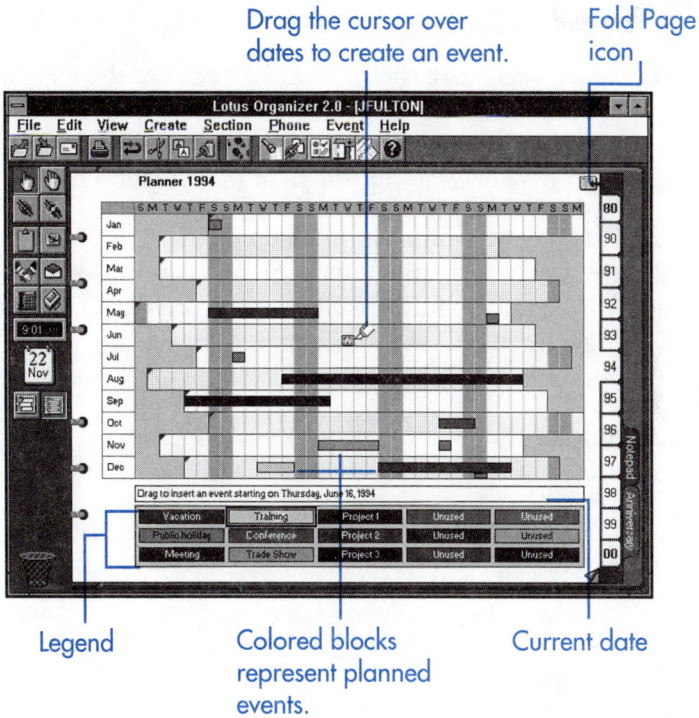

Legend

Colored blocks
represent planned
events.

Current date

Figure 16.1 The Planner section.

Note that the current date is displayed in the text box
that runs along the bottom of the chart. As you move the
mouse over the chart, the date changes to reflect the position of the mouse pointer. To select another year, click on
one of the year tabs displayed along the right border of the
Planner.

Adding Events

Although there are at least two ways to place a planned
event on your chart, we'll focus on the Planner's unique
method because it's the simplest and fastest way to go. It's a
little like the drag-and-drop methods described in previous
lessons.

Follow these steps to add an event to your Planner:

1. When you move the mouse pointer over the legend at the base of the chart, it changes to look like a marker tip. Click once on any colored block in the legend. (For example, click on the Vacation block.)

2. Drag over the dates for which you want to plan the event. For example, to plan your vacation from July 3–10, click on July 3rd and drag to July 10th. As you drag, the dates take on the same color as the block you selected from the legend.

3. Release the mouse button. Your event appears on the Planner.

You can add additional features to an event with the Edit Event dialog box. See the next section for help.

You can change your view of events with the View icons. There is a View icon that enables you to see a quarter of a year, and one that enables you to see the full year.

Editing an Event

To edit an event, double-click on it, and the Edit Event dialog box appears (see Figure 16.2).

In the Edit Event dialog box, you can change the event type, start or end date, and duration. Some additional options are only available through this dialog box:

Notes   Add a description for the event.

Row   Change the row (1–4) in which the event appears.

Categories   Select a category for the event. When the event appears in your Calendar, it will bear this category icon.

Book free time   When selected, this option causes
the Planner to block out the entire day in your Calendar for the event.

Confidential   If you share your files, you can keep
this event confidential.

Alarm, Repeat, or Cost   You can set an alarm for an
event, make it automatically repeat (such as every
month), and associate a cost to the event. Follow the
steps in Lesson 8 for adding these extras.

You can add an event with this dialog box if you want,
and then add these options and the event in one step. Just
double-click on a date to open the Create Event dialog box,
and then make your selections to add an event.

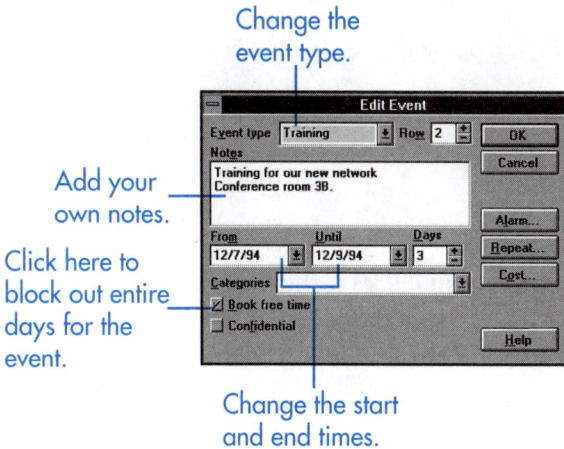

Change the
event type.

Add your
own notes.

Click here to
block out entire
days for the
event.

Change the start
and end times.

Figure 16.2   The Edit Event dialog box.

Quick Change Artist   You can move an
event by clicking on it and dragging it. Move the
start or end date (and hence, the duration) of an
event by dragging just one end.

Using the Planner with the Calendar

Conceivably, you could double-book yourself if you made a Calendar appointment and planned an event for the same day. To avoid this, display your events in the Calendar:

1. Open the Section menu and select Show Through, or click on the Show Through button on the SmartIcon palette. The Show Through dialog box, shown in Figure 16.3, appears.

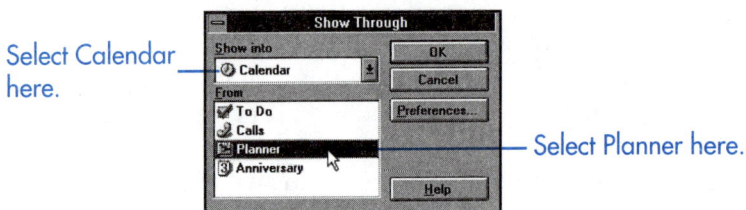

Select Calendar here.

Select Planner here.

Figure 16.3 The Show Through dialog box.

2. From the Show into drop-down list box, select Calendar.

3. In the From drop-down list box, select Planner.

4. If you want, you can click on the Preferences button and choose where to display the Planner events, as well as how much information to display. Make your selections and click on OK to return to the Show Through dialog box.

5. Click on OK. Your Planner events appear with your appointments in the Calendar.

In this lesson, you learned how to use the Planner. In the next lesson, you'll learn how to use Organizer's Notepad section to help you organize your notes.

Lesson 17

Using the Notepad to Make a Note for Yourself

In this lesson, you'll learn how to use Organizer's Notepad to keep track of important text.

What Is the Notepad?

Organizer's Notepad is a computerized replacement for a pad of paper. You can note information that takes up more space than a single page. You can also place graphics (such as maps, charts, and graphs) into your notes. You can even import financial information from a spreadsheet such as Lotus 1-2-3. You can use the Notepad to document thoughts, methods, and even events.

Notepad considers all pages to be part of one single blank pad of paper, and adds new pages as though it were adding a new chapter to a book. Your Notepad will even build a table of contents for you as you add pages. You create new chapters as necessary to group like pages together.

Creating Notepad Pages

When you create a page, you can type text or import information from another source. To create a Notepad page:

1. Click on the Notepad tab to access the Notepad section.

2. Double-click on the Contents page or press Insert. The Create Page dialog box appears (see Figure 17.1).

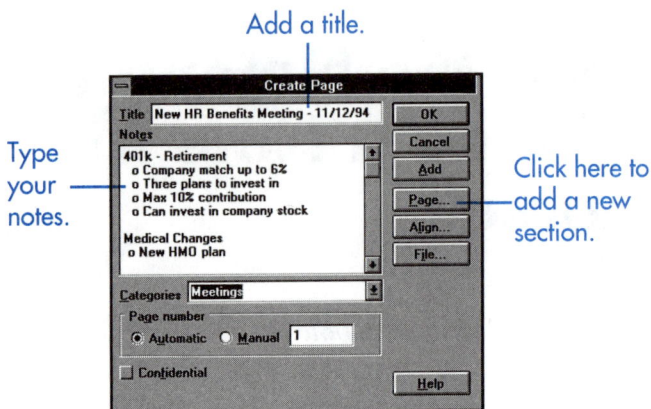

Add a title.

Type your notes.

Click here to add a new section.

Figure 17.1 The Create Page dialog box.

3. If you want to start a new section of notes (a chapter), click on the Page button and select the Start a chapter check box from the dialog box that appears. Then click on OK to return to the Create Page dialog box.

4. Type a title for this page if you like.

5. Type your notes. If you want to import information, see the section "Importing Information into Notepad" for help.

6. Select a category, assign a manual page number, or make your note confidential if you want.

7. Click on OK to save your note.

Moving Through the Notepad

Once you have entered a few notes, you can move among them freely, and you can reorder them if you like. First, go to the Contents page of the Notepad section (shown in Figure 17.2) by clicking on the Notepad tab.

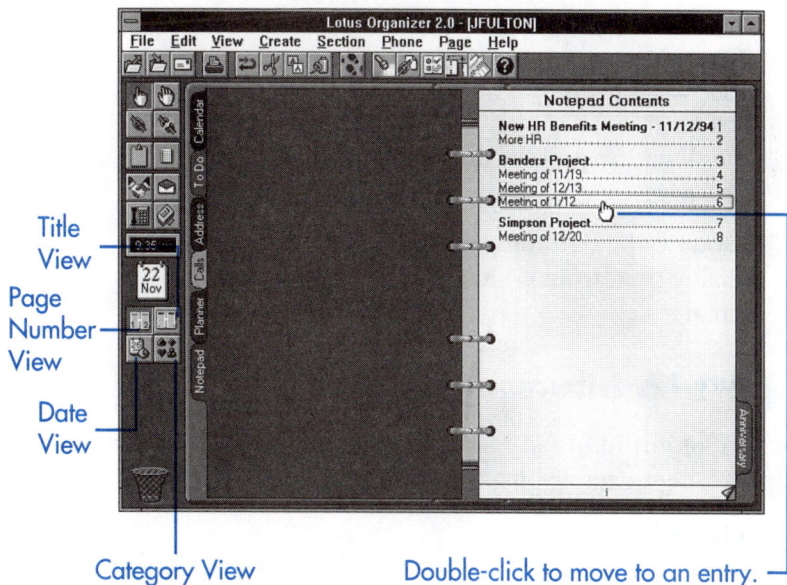

Figure 17.2 The Contents page.

From there, perform one of these steps:

- To move to a particular page, double-click on it.

- To move from page to page, click on the turned-back page corners at the bottom of each page.

- To reorder a page, click on it and drag it to its new location on the Contents page. You can use this technique to add a new page to a previous chapter (create the page, and then drag it to the chapter in which it belongs).

Moving through the Notepad might be easier if your pages are in a different order. For example, you can sort your Notepad pages by category, date, or title simply by clicking on the appropriate View icon. To switch back to page order, click on the Page Number View icon.

Editing Notepad Pages

To make changes to a page, move to the page you want to change and do one of the following:

- Click on the page to make changes to the text on the page.

- Double-click on the page to display the Edit Page dialog box, from which you can make other changes.

Importing Information into Notepad

You can import information, including text, graphics, charts, or spreadsheet data, from another source.

Sideways Size   You can flip a page sideways to display spreadsheet data or other horizontal information. From the Create/Edit Page dialog box, click on Page, and then click on Folded.

Importing a Text or Bitmap File

You can import a text file or a graphics file (bitmap file) by following these steps:

1. In Notepad, press Insert to access the Create Page dialog box.

2. From the Create Page dialog box, click on File. The File dialog box appears.

3. If necessary, change to a different drive or directory.

4. From the List files of type drop-down list box, select the type of file you want to import.

5. Under File name, type the name of the file you want to import.

6. Click on OK. The file is imported into the Create Page dialog box.

7. Click on OK to return to Organizer.

Copying or Linking Other Information

You can copy or link information from any Windows program. This can be any type of information, such as formatted text, a chart, a graphic picture, or spreadsheet data.

You copy information using an area of memory called the Clipboard. You copy the data to this Clipboard, and then paste it into a Notepad page.

If you prefer, you can link information instead of copying it. A *link* keeps your data updated. If you change the data in the original application (for example, if you change your spreadsheet figures), those figures are automatically updated in Organizer through this link. (The application that contains the original file you are linking must support the link function—called DDE—in order for you to use it.)

To link information, follow these steps:

1. Open the file that contains information you want to copy to Notepad.

2. Select the information, open the Edit menu, and then select Copy to copy it to the Clipboard.

3. Switch to Organizer. Move to the Notepad section by clicking on the Notepad tab.

4. Press Insert to create a new page.

5. Open the Edit menu and select Paste Special. Select a format type that matches the information you want to paste. Choose Bitmap to paste graphics, Text to paste text, or Metafile to paste data that combines text and graphics.

6. Click on Paste if you want to copy the data into Notepad. Click on Paste link if you want to link the data instead.

7. Click on OK to close the Create Page dialog box and return to Notepad.

Deleting Notepad Pages

Deleting Notepad pages (or a series of pages) is the same as deleting anything in Organizer: you simply drag-and-drop them from the Contents page into the Trash basket. After you've thrown away the page(s), some flames in the Trash flare up, signifying that you've successfully trashed a page.

In this lesson, you learned how to work with Organizer's Notepad. In the next lesson, you'll learn how to record anniversaries.

18

Working with Anniversaries

In this lesson, you'll learn how to fill Organizer's Anniversary section with information about personal and business anniversaries.

What Is an Anniversary?

Everyone—and I mean everyone—forgets an anniversary now and then! (Let's hope that the one you forget belongs to someone else.) With Lotus Organizer, you don't have to blow off those important dates anymore. You can keep a special diary of anniversaries. In fact, with Organizer's Anniversary section, you can track any event that recurs annually (birthdays, trade shows, office parties, and so on).

The handiest thing about the Anniversary section is the fact that you can review anniversaries on a monthly basis— you don't have to check the Anniversary section every day. The capability to see all anniversaries for an entire month at a glance is the single biggest benefit to using the Anniversary section over using the Calendar section. The Anniversary section is made up of a dozen lists (each of which represents a different month). The entries you make in the Anniversary section show up in your Calendar section along with your appointments.

Adding an Anniversary

To add an anniversary to your Anniversary section:

1. Click on the Anniversary tab to move to the Anniversary section.

2. Double-click on the month in which you want to add your anniversary. The Create Anniversary dialog box appears, as shown in Figure 18.1.

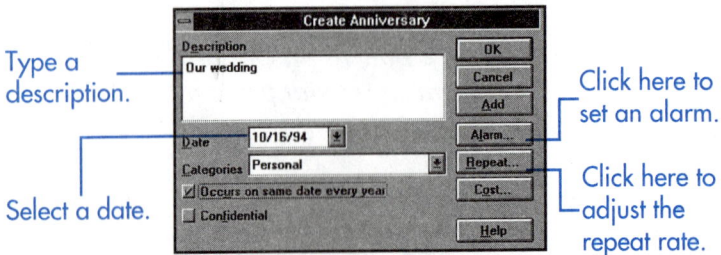

Figure 18.1 The Create Anniversary dialog box.

3. In the Description text box, type the text that will serve as a description for this anniversary. Your description text can contain up to 256 characters.

4. Under Date, click on the down arrow button to choose a date from the calendar display. Change months in the calendar display by clicking on either black arrow. Select a day of the month by clicking on that day's number.

5. If your anniversary repeats annually, click on Occurs on same date every year. Otherwise, click on the Repeat button to open the Repeat dialog box (see Figure 18.2). Select a repeat type and frequency, and select a duration. Click on OK to return to the Create Anniversary dialog box. (For more information on repeating items, see Lesson 8.)

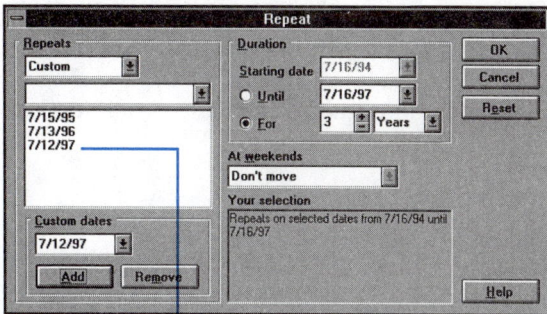

Add custom dates for an event that repeats on the same Saturday every year, for example.

Figure 18.2   The Repeat dialog box.

6. If you want to be reminded of your anniversary, click on Alarm. The Alarm dialog box opens (see Figure 18.3). Set the number of minutes that you want the alarm to go off in advance of the anniversary. Select a tune to play or type a message to display if you want. Click on OK to return to the Create Anniversary dialog box. (For more information on setting alarms, see Lesson 8.)

7. Click on the OK button to add your Anniversary text to Organizer's Anniversary section.

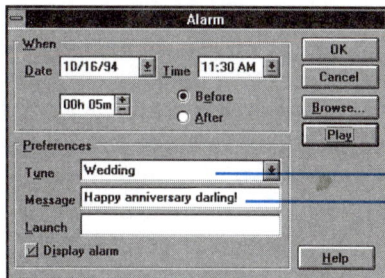

Select a tune or type a message.

Figure 18.3   The Alarm dialog box.

Displaying Your Anniversaries in the Calendar Section

Your anniversaries do not appear in any other section until you make them. To do that:

1. Open the Section menu.

2. Select Show Through. The Show Through dialog box appears.

3. From the Show into drop-down list, select Calendar.

4. Under From, select Anniversary.

5. Click on OK.

Now, if you switch to the Calendar section, you'll see your anniversaries displayed on the proper date. This saves you the trouble of remembering to check the Anniversary section all the time.

Changing an Anniversary

There may come a time when you find an Anniversary entry is inaccurate for one reason or another. To fix these inaccuracies, you can change the text in the description of any anniversary. You can also change the date or the repeat rate of any anniversary. Here's how:

1. Double-click on the anniversary that you want to change. The Edit Anniversary dialog box opens.

2. If you want to change the date, click on the down arrow button next to the Anniversary on text box and choose a new date. If you want to change the description text, click inside the Description text box and change your text. You can also change the repeat rate and/or add an alarm.

3. Click on OK when you're through.

Your Anniversary section displays your changes. If you've changed the date, you may have to flip through the pages to the new month in order to see the anniversary.

Deleting an Anniversary

On occasion, you might have to delete anniversaries. Here's how:

1. Click on the Anniversary tab to open the Anniversary section.

2. Navigate to the anniversary you want to delete.

3. Drag-and-drop the defunct anniversary onto the Trash basket icon.

> **Oops, That Was My Wedding Anniversary!** If you accidently delete an anniversary you need, immediately select Edit, Undo Anniversary Delete to restore it.

In this lesson, you learned how to work with your Anniversary section. In the next lesson, you'll learn how to print information in your Organizer file.

Lesson

Printing

In this lesson, you'll learn about printing the information in your Organizer files.

Printing Sections of the Organizer

Organizer lets you print the contents of your different sections, which means you can have actual hard copy pages to insert into your day planner or you can generate mailing labels. The process of printing from all of Organizer's sections is fairly universal. You can use the same dialog box to print each of the sections.

To print a section, follow these instructions:

1. Select Print from the File menu, or click on the Print icon in the SmartIcon palette. The Print dialog box opens, as shown in Figure 19.1.

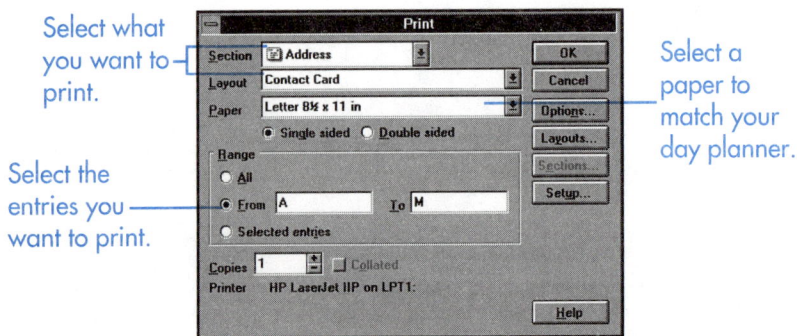

Select what you want to print.

Select the entries you want to print.

Select a paper to match your day planner.

Figure 19.1 The Print dialog box.

2. In the Section drop-down list box, choose the section you want to print.

3. Select a Layout. Some layouts combine information from several sections.

4. In the Paper drop-down list box, select the paper size you will be using. You can also use this option to print sections for a specific brand of day planner, such as Day Timer or Franklin Day Planner. If you want to customize the paper size/page layout, see Lesson 20.

5. Select either Single sided or Double sided printing.

6. Click on the All option button to print all records in this section. If you want to limit printing to a range of names (Address or Notepad) or dates (Calendar, Planner, and so on), click on the From option button and type a range of names or dates.

7. In the Copies text box, type the number of copies you want.

8. If you selected a layout that combines information from several sources, you can click on the Sections button and map where you want specific sections placed on the page.

9. Select OK. Organizer prints the specified section.

Be Specific!   If you want to print a specific address, appointment, or Notepad page, you can just drag-and-drop it onto the Print icon in the Toolbox.

Other Print Options

There are many other options you can select before printing. Here are the ones you'll find when you click on the Options button in the Print dialog box:

- **Skip blank pages**   Have Organizer skip pages that are blank (and not print them).

- **Print in black & white**   Use this option to print in black and white on a color printer.

- **Print order**   Select the order in which you want your items to print on a multicolumn page.

- **Double-sided**   You can select to print on both sides of a perforated paper if you want (i.e., four pages at once).

    To select the following options, you must click on the Layouts button instead:

- **Portrait vs. Landscape orientation**   Portrait orientation prints parallel to the width (as in 8 1/2" × 11") while landscape orientation prints parallel to the length of a page (as in 11" × 8 1/2").

- **Print first line only, print icons, or print monthly calendars**   Select any of these additional options found in the Layouts dialog box.

Printing Labels

Organizer comes equipped to print standard label formats to suit the most readily available label stock. However, you can only print labels from the Address section. That's because label printing really doesn't make sense when you're working with (for example) a chart in the Planner section.

    Here's how you print labels:

1. Select Print from the File menu, or click on the Print icon in the Toolbox. The Print dialog box opens. (See Figure 19.2.)

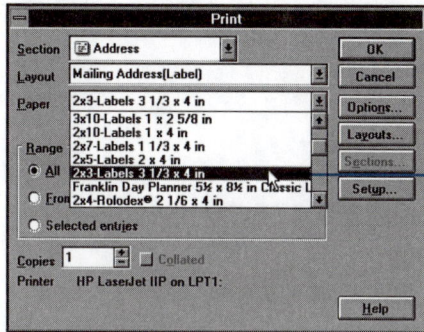

Select a
label type.

Figure 19.2 Printing labels.

2. Select the Address section.

3. Under Layout, select Mailing Address (Label).

4. Under Paper, select a label size.

> **Don't Settle for Less** You can customize
> any label's layout if you want. Check out Lesson
> 20 for more on creating customized label
> layouts.

5. Click on the All option button to print all address
records. If you want to limit printing to a range of
names, click on the From option button and type in
a range of names.

6. To print more than one copy of each label, click on
Options. Under Labels, select the number of copies
to print. Click on OK to return to the Print dialog
box.

7. Click on OK to begin printing labels.

In this lesson, you learned how to print. In the next
lesson, you'll learn how to customize the layout of your
page.

Lesson 20

Customizing Page Layout

In this lesson, you'll learn how to customize Organizer's pages. You'll also learn how to select a font and prepare a label's layout to suit your own needs.

Choosing a Page Layout

Organizer comes equipped with several page layout formats that match those of common paper products available in office supply stores. You can, however, create customized page layouts for any Organizer information you want to print.

To change the page layout, follow these steps:

1. From the Print dialog box, click on the Layouts button. The Layouts dialog box opens. (To access the Print dialog box, click on the Print SmartIcon.)

2. Click on Paper. The Paper dialog box, shown in Figure 20.1, appears.

3. Choose the options you want from the dialog box.

4. If you want to create a new page layout instead of changing an existing one, type a new Name and click on Add.

5. Click on the OK button twice to save your page layout and return to the Print dialog box.

Type the name of
your new layout.

Change the number and
size of rows and columns.

Change
the size of
a label by
dragging
its
borders.

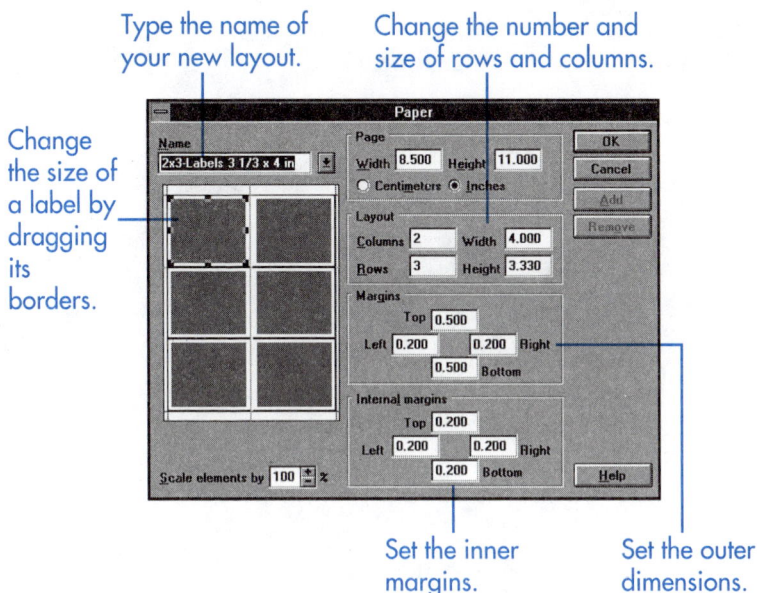

Set the inner
margins.

Set the outer
dimensions.

Figure 20.1   The Paper dialog box.

Selecting a Font

Sometimes, you choose a font based on personal preference;
other times, the font you use is determined by your department or business system. For whatever reason, you'll probably need to know how to change the fonts you use in
Organizer. You can use any font that's installed on your
computer.

Here's how you select a font:

1. After you've selected what you want to print from
the Print dialog box, click on the Layouts button.
The Layouts dialog box appears.

2. Click on the Styles button. The Styles dialog box
appears.

3. Select the element whose font you want to change.

4. Click on the Font button. The Font dialog box, shown in Figure 20.2, appears.

Select a font and size.

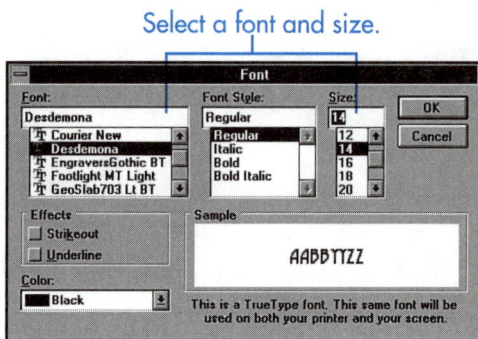

Figure 20.2   The Font dialog box.

5. Select a Font and Size. If you want, select a Font Style and/or Color.

6. Click on OK to return to the Styles dialog box.

7. Select another element to change if you want, and repeat steps 4-6.

8. Click on OK twice to return to the Print dialog box. Click on OK again to print your information.

In this lesson, you learned how to customize the page layout and change the font of any text element. In the next lesson, you'll learn how to customize the various sections of Organizer.

Lesson

Customizing Sections

In this lesson, you'll learn how to customize your various Organizer sections, such as the Calendar, To Do List, and Address sections.

Customizing Organizer Sections

You can personalize each Organizer section by changing its settings. For example, you can select the amount of information to display. You can select from other options too. For example, under Calendar, you can customize the start and end times of the days or the default time slot length. In the To Do section, you can customize the status color of items, and you can set it up to automatically delete completed tasks for you.

Here's how you customize an Organizer section:

1. Click on the tab whose section you want to customize.

2. Open the View menu and select Preferences. The Preferences dialog box appropriate to that section appears. Figure 21.1 shows the Calendar Preferences dialog box.

Control what information is displayed.

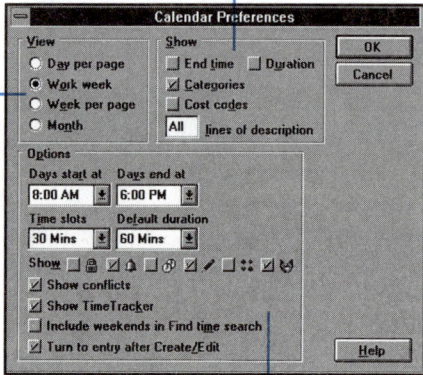

Select these same options with a View icon.

Select additional options.

Figure 21.1   A typical Preferences dialog box.

3. Change any option you like. Under View, you'll find the same options that you can select by simply clicking on a View icon. Under Show, you'll find options that control how much information is displayed for a typical entry in that section. Under Options, you'll find other options specific to that section, such as the display of optional symbols like the Alarm symbol.

4. Click on OK to save your changes.

Changing the Color, Name, and Appearance of Sections

You can also customize the look of each section by changing its color, name, and appearance. Here's how:

1. Open the Section menu and select Customize, or click on the Section Customize button on the SmartIcon palette. The Customize dialog box, shown in Figure 21.2, appears.

Move a section by clicking Up or Down.

Rename the
section if you
want.

Select a new color in this section.

Figure 21.2 The Customize dialog box.

2. Under Tabs, select the section you want to customize.

3. To move a section to a different location within Organizer, click on the Up or Down button.

4. Change the color of a section's tab by selecting one from the Color list.

5. To change a section's name, click on the Rename button and type a new name. Click OK to return to the Customize dialog box.

6. Click on OK when you're through.

Is That All?   You can add new sections (based on the style of an existing section) by clicking on Add. To remove a section you don't use, select it from the list and click on Remove.

Adding Pictures

You can add pizzazz to your Organizer by selecting customized pictures for the tabs. And it's really simple, too! To add a picture to a section:

1. Open the Section menu and select Customize, or click on the Section Customize button on the SmartIcon palette.

2. Select the section to which you want to add a picture and click on Picture. The Picture dialog box appears (see Figure 21.3).

Type a file name or use Browse to locate it.

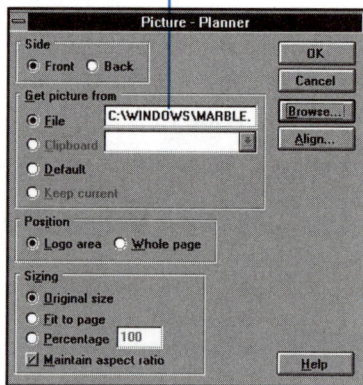

Figure 21.3 The Picture dialog box.

3. Choose whether you want your picture to appear at the front or back of the section.

4. Select the location of the picture. If you've copied a picture to the Clipboard, select that. If your picture is in a file, select File, and then click on Browse and select the file from the list.

5. Click on Logo area to display your picture on just the tab; click on Whole page to display it on the full page.

6. If you want, you can adjust the size of the image with the Sizing options.

7. Click on Align and change the alignment of the image (to center it, for example).

8. Click on OK twice. Your picture appears in that section.

Displaying Information from Other Sections

You can display entries from other sections in the current section. For example, you can set up your Calendar to show the entries you made in the Anniversary section, so you can remind yourself of an anniversary while you're scheduling an appointment.

Here's how you customize one section to see information from other sections:

1. Open the Section menu and select Show Through, or click on the Show Through button on the SmartIcon palette. The Show Through dialog box appears (see Figure 21.4).

Select the section to customize.

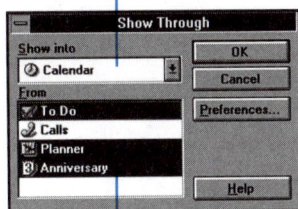

Select the sections whose information you want to show in the current section.

Figure 21.4 The Show Through dialog box.

2. Under Show into, select the section you want to customize. For example, select Calendar.

3. Under From, select the sections whose entries you want to show in this section. You can select more than one section if you want. For example, select the To Do and Anniversary sections.

4. If you want, click on Preferences and indicate whether to include your entries before or after the regular entries in this section. Click on OK to return to the Show Through dialog box.

5. Click on OK.

Now, if you followed the example, you'll see entries from the To Do and Anniversary sections in your Calendar. Calendar displays entries from other sections in a different color from your appointment text so you can easily distinguish them.

In this lesson, you learned about customizing your various Organizer sections. In the next lesson, you'll learn how to customize Organizer itself.

22

Customizing Organizer

In this lesson, you'll learn how to customize your Organizer binder, how to load a startup file, and how to automatically save your file periodically.

Putting Your Name on Your Organizer

You should take a moment to personalize your Organizer. Since Organizer is intended to imitate the traditional daily planner, your name should go on the front cover for all to see. You have seven lines of text space to work with. Follow these steps to put your name on your Organizer:

1. Open the Organizer file so the front page of the binder is showing.

2. Place the insertion point in the name tag area.

3. Type the name you want to appear on the front of the binder. You can use arrow keys, the Spacebar, and the Delete key to navigate around the name tag while you're personalizing.

4. When you're finished, select Save from the File menu.

Changing the Color of the Binder

If you're the kind of person who just has to see software display your favorite colors, you're in luck. You can change the color of the binder to suit your personal preference. In addition, you can add a texture to the binder, such as silk or leather.

This is how you change the color and/or texture of Organizer's binder:

1. Choose Customize from the Section menu, or click on the Customize Section button on the SmartIcon palette. The Customize dialog box opens, as shown in Figure 22.1.

Customize your binder with
fun textures and colors.   Select a color.

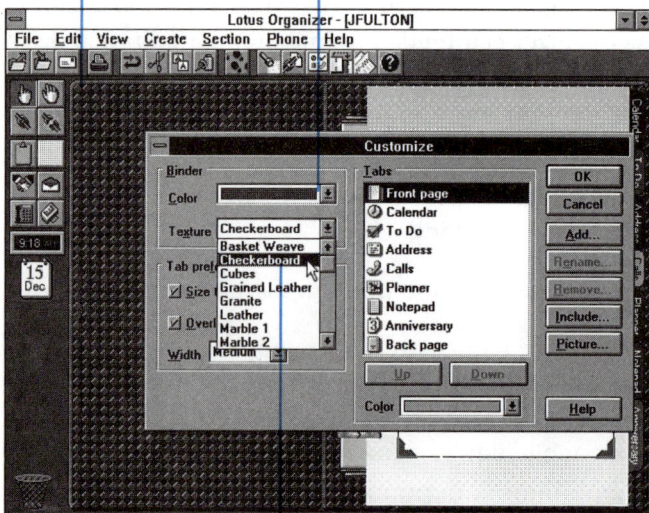

Select a texture.

Figure 22.1   The Customize dialog box.

2. In the Binder area, click on the arrow under Color, and then select a color from the palette.

3. If you want, select a Texture from the drop-down list.

4. Click on OK.

Your binder is now the color and/or texture you chose. The same color and texture will be displayed when you open the Organizer file again.

Loading Your Organizer File Automatically

If you use only one Organizer file, or if you use one file more often than others, you should set up Organizer to load that file automatically. To do so, follow these steps:

1. Open the File menu and select Organizer Preferences.

2. Select Organizer Setup. The Organizer Setup dialog box appears (see Figure 22.2).

Type the name of the file you want
Organizer to open automatically.

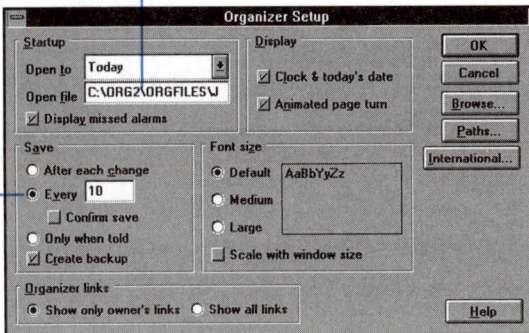

You can save your file periodically
with these options.

Figure 22.2   The Organizer Setup dialog box.

3. In the Open file text box, type the path and file name of your Organizer file, or click on the Browse button and select your file from the list.

4. Click on OK.

Your file loads automatically for you every time you start Organizer.

Saving Your Organizer File Automatically

You can set up Organizer so that it saves your file periodically as you work. That way, even if something should happen to cause your PC to temporarily lose power, you won't lose any of your changes.

To change your Organizer setup:

1. Open the File menu and select Organizer Preferences.

2. Select Organizer Setup. The Organizer Setup dialog box appears, as shown in Figure 22.2.

3. Under Save, select either After each change or Every.

4. If you selected Every in step 3, enter a number of minutes in the text box. For example, if you enter **10**, Organizer will automatically save your file every 10 minutes.

5. If you want to confirm the save before it happens, click on Confirm save.

6. Click on OK.

In this lesson, you learned how to customize Organizer's binder and set up Organizer's automatic file loading and saving features to suit your own needs. In the next lesson, you'll learn how to set up a password to protect your Organizer file.

Lesson

Using a Password

In this lesson, you'll learn how to set and change a password.

Establishing a Password

Organizer helps you keep unauthorized people from viewing and changing your Organizer files. You maintain this level of security with Organizer's password protection feature. Here's how to establish a password:

1. Open an Organizer file.

2. Open the File menu and select Organizer Preferences. Select User Access. The User Access dialog box appears.

3. Click on the Password button. The Password dialog box opens, as shown in Figure 23.1.

Figure 23.1 The Password dialog box.

4. Type your password into the Password text box. Notice that Organizer substitutes asterisks for the characters you type to prevent clandestine on-lookers from learning your password.

Be Careful! Organizer's passwords are case-sensitive. If you establish a password with any uppercase letters, you'll have to uppercase those same letters every time you enter your password.

5. Click on the OK button, and then retype the same information into the Verify Password dialog box.

6. Click on the OK button to return to the User Access dialog box.

7. Click on OK to return to Organizer.

You now have password protection for information maintained in any of your Organizer sections. You'll be asked to enter a password the next time you open your file.

Limiting User Access

In addition to using password protection, if you are on a network, there are five levels of access you can assign to your co-workers so you can limit what they can see and/or do to your file. To set up those limits, follow these steps:

1. Open the File menu and select Organizer Preferences. Select User Access. The User Access dialog box, shown in Figure 23.2, appears.

2. Click on the Names button. Select a user to whom you want to give access to your file. Click Add to add the user. Repeat to add additional users. Click Close when you're through.

3. Under People or groups, select the name of the user whose access level you want to adjust. By default, users you've selected in step 2 can see only your available free time.

Select a user...

...then select an access level.

Figure 23.2 The User Access dialog box.

4. Select an access level for the user:

None   No access.

Free time   The user can view only your available time slots.

Reader   In addition to free time access, the user can read your Organizer file.

Assistant   In addition to free time and reader access, the user can write (make changes) to your file. Assistants can also schedule meetings for you and change preferences.

Trustee   In addition to free time, reader, and assistant access, the user can customize your file.

Owner   In addition to free time, reader, assistant, and trustee access, the user can read confidential information and change other users' access levels.

5. Repeat steps 3 and 4 to change the access level of another user.

6. When you're through, click on OK.

In this lesson, you learned how to set and change a password. In the next lesson, you'll learn how to establish links to information in another section of Organizer.

Lesson 24

Using Links to Cross-Reference Information

In this lesson, you'll learn how to keep information updated automatically (linked) between sections of your Organizer files and with the files of other applications.

What Are Links?

Links are connections between Organizer sections. Organizer enables you to cross-reference (link) information maintained by some sections of Organizer. You can use these links to quickly jump to a certain Notepad page or a specific entry in your Address book. Links provide a neat way to see related information in other Organizer sections or another application's files. You can set up a whole network of linked information.

> **Show Through Instead**   Instead of linking information in various sections, you can display information from one section in another with the Show Through command. (See Lesson 21.)

Setting Up Links

You have to set up a link before you can use it to quickly jump to another Organizer section's information or another

application's file. Here's how you set up a link betweeen two
Organizer sections:

1. Open the Organizer section that holds the information you want to link to information elsewhere.

2. Click on the Link button in the Toolbox (it looks
like a link of chain). When you click on the Link
button, a chain icon appears next to your mouse
pointer.

3. Click on the information you want to link. Figure
24.1 shows an example of information selected for
linking.

Select the item to link to.

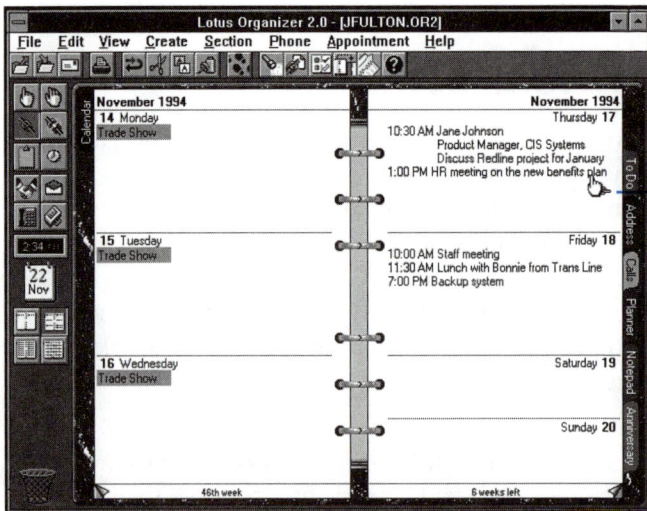

Figure 24.1   The chain signifies the first part of the link.

4. Navigate to the information that will comprise the
other end of the link. In Figure 24.2, I've selected
some notes in the Notepad section.

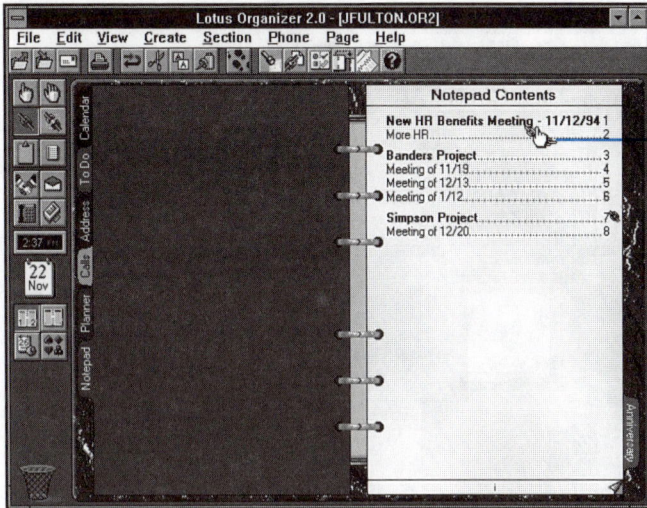

Select the item to link.

Figure 24.2 Select the information that is the other end of the link.

5. Click on the information you want to link. Organizer displays a link of chain near the linked information to signify that a link has been established
(see Figure 24.3).

To see your newly linked information, point to the Link
icon and hold down the left mouse button. To jump to the
other end of your link, click on any item listed on the Link
menu.

Multiple Links You can link multiple entries
to one entry if you want; simply repeat the steps
here over and over. You can also press Ctrl when
you click on the Link button, and you can click on
multiple entries to link to your first item. Click on the Link
button again to return to a normal cursor.

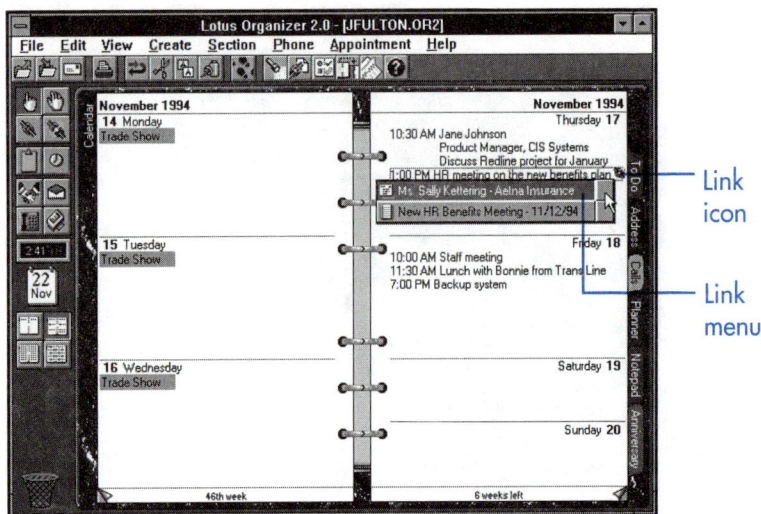

Figure 24.3   The Link icon.

To delete a link, simply click on the Unlink tool (it looks like a broken chain), and then click on the Link icon you want to delete.

Using Information from Other Applications

You can link information in one of your sections with other applications' files. You could, for example, open a spreadsheet file that relates to a meeting described in an appointment.

Here's how you establish a link to another application's file:

1. Click on the information you want to link.

2. Open the Create menu and select File Link, or click on the Create a Link button on the SmartIcon palette. The File Link dialog box opens (see Figure 24.4).

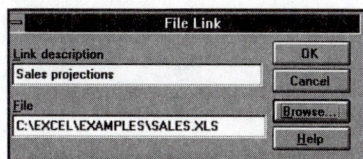

Figure 24.4   The File Link dialog box.

3. In the Link description text box, type the name you want to use as a label for this link.

4. If you know the name of the file that contains the information that will comprise the other end of your link, type it into the File text box. If you don't know the exact path and file name, click on the Browse button to search for it.

5. Click on OK.

Your link is established. A Link icon appears near the Organizer information that you linked. To see your new external link as it's listed on the Link menu, point to the Link icon and hold down the left mouse button. Linked application files are represented on the Link menu by a small diskette icon and the name of the file. To jump to the other end of your link, move the pointer over the link information, and release the left mouse button. To see what you typed into the Reference dialog box, move the pointer over the ellipsis (...) at the end of the Link menu item and release the mouse button.

In this lesson, you learned about linking information between Organizer's sections and linking information created by external applications. This is the last lesson in the *10 Minute Guide to Lotus Organizer 2.0*. Have fun using Organizer!

Overtime

Appendix

Microsoft Windows Primer

Microsoft Windows is a graphical interface program that makes your computer easier to use by enabling you to select menu items and pictures instead of typing commands. Before you can take advantage of it, however, you must learn some Windows basics.

Starting Microsoft Windows

To start Windows, do the following:

1. At the DOS prompt, type WIN.

2. Press Enter.

The Windows title screen appears for a few moments, and then you see a screen like the one in Figure A.1.

What If Windows Didn't Start? You may have to change to the Windows directory before starting Windows; to do so, type CD\WINDOWS and press Enter. Then type WIN and press Enter again.

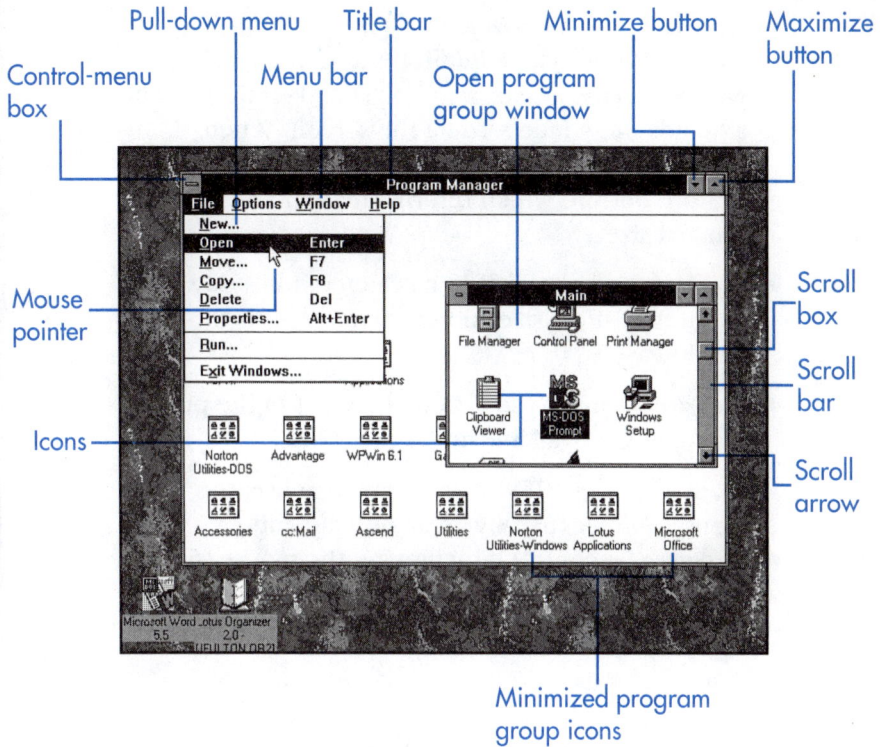

Pull-down menu   Title bar   Minimize button   Maximize button

Control-menu box   Menu bar   Open program group window

Mouse pointer

Icons

Scroll box

Scroll bar

Scroll arrow

Minimized program group icons

Figure A.1   The Windows Program Manager.

Parts of a Windows Screen

As shown in Figure A.1, the Windows screen contains several unique elements that you won't see in DOS. Here's a brief summary.

- *Title bar*   Shows the name of the window or program.

- *Program group windows*   Contain program icons that allow you to run programs.

- *Icons*   Graphic representations of programs. To run a program, you select its icon.

- *Minimize and Maximize buttons* Alter a window's size. The Minimize button shrinks the window to the size of an icon. The Maximize button expands the window to fill the screen. When maximized, a window contains a double-arrow Restore button, which returns the window to its original size.

- *Control-menu box* When selected, pulls down a menu that offers size and location controls for the window.

- *Pull-down menu bar* Contains a list of the pull-down menus available in the program.

- *Mouse pointer* If you are using a mouse, the mouse pointer (usually an arrow) appears on-screen. You control it by moving the mouse (discussed later in this appendix).

- *Scroll bars* If a window contains more information than can be displayed in the window, a scroll bar appears. *Scroll arrows* on each end of the scroll bar allow you to scroll slowly. The *scroll box* allows you to scroll more quickly.

The Organizer program contains many of these same elements. Look for them after you start the program in Lesson 1.

Using a Mouse

To work most efficiently in Windows, you should use a mouse. You can press mouse buttons and move the mouse in various ways to change the way it acts:

Point means to move the mouse pointer onto the specified item by moving the mouse. The tip of the mouse pointer must be touching the item.

Click on an item means to move the pointer onto the specified item and press the mouse button once. Unless specified otherwise, use the left mouse button.

Double-click on an item means to move the pointer onto the specified item and press and release the left mouse button twice quickly.

Drag means to move the mouse pointer onto the specified item, hold down the left mouse button, and move the mouse while holding down the button.

You can use the mouse to perform common Windows activities, including running applications and moving and resizing windows.

Starting a Program

To start a program, simply double-click its icon. If its icon is contained in a program group window that's not open at the moment, open the window first. Follow these steps:

1. If necessary, open the program group window that contains the program you want to run. For example, to start Organizer, open the Lotus Applications program group. To open a program group window, double-click on its icon.

2. Double-click on the icon for the program you want to run. For example, double-click on the Organizer 2.0 icon.

Using Menus

Like all Windows programs, Organizer contains a pull-down menu bar (see Figure A.2) from which you can select commands. Each Windows program that you run has a set of pull-down menus; Windows itself has a set too.

To open a menu, click on its name on the menu bar. Once a menu is open, you can select a command from it by clicking on the desired command. To close a menu without selecting a command, click inside the document or press Esc.

Accelerator Keys Notice that in Figure A.2, some commands are followed by key names such as Ins. These are called *accelerator keys*. You can use these keys to perform the commands without even opening the menu.

Plain English

Grayed-out commands are unavailable.

A command with an arrow opens a cascading menu.

Accelerator keys activate a command even when the menu is not open.

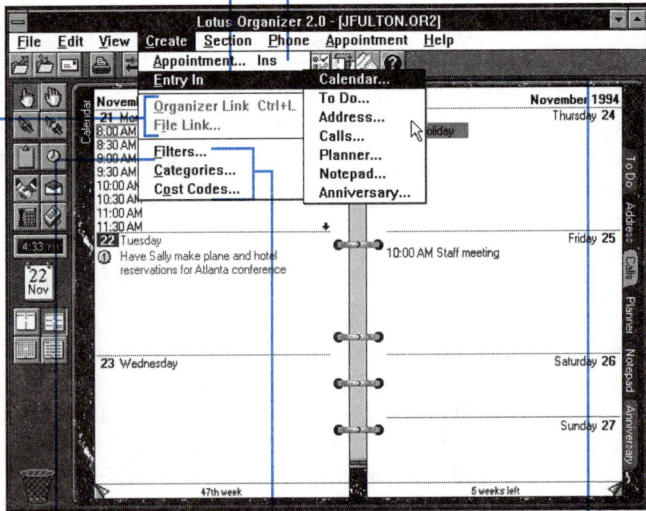

Press the selection (underlined) letter when the menu is open to activate a command.

A command with an ellipsis opens a dialog box.

The currently selected command is highlighted.

Figure A.2 A menu lists various commands you can perform.

Usually, when you select a command, the command is performed immediately. However:

- If the command name is gray (rather than black), the command is unavailable at the moment and you cannot choose it.

- If the command name is followed by an arrow, selecting the command will cause a submenu to appear, from which you select another command.

- If the command name is followed by an ellipsis (three dots), selecting it will cause a dialog box to appear. You'll learn about dialog boxes in the next section.

Pop-up Menus   Organizer 2.0 offers fast access to common menu commands through pop-up menus. Simply move the mouse pointer over an area you want to work on, and then click the right mouse button. A pop-up menu appears with commands specific to the object to which you were pointing. Select a command from the pop-up menu by clicking on it.

Navigating Dialog Boxes

A dialog box is Windows' way of requesting additional information. Organizer is no exception. Figure A.3 depicts common dialog box elements.

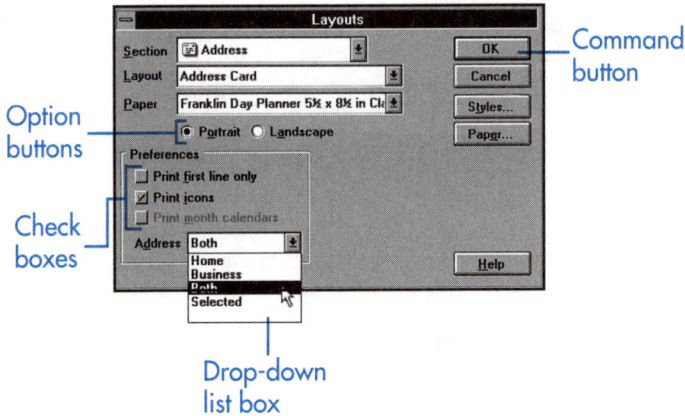

Figure A.3 A typical dialog box.

Each dialog box contains one or more of the following elements:

- *List boxes* display available choices. To activate a list, click inside the list box. If the entire list is not visible, use the scroll bar to view the items in the list. To select an item from the list, click on it, or if a text box is provided, type in your selection.

- *Drop-down lists* are similar to list boxes, but only one item in the list is shown. To see the rest of the items, you must open the list. Click on the down arrow on the right side of the drop-down list and hold down the mouse button. Drag down the list to select an item, and then release the mouse button.

- *Text boxes* enable you to type an entry. To activate a text box, click inside it. To edit an existing entry, use the arrow keys to move the cursor, and use the Del or Backspace keys to delete existing characters. Then type your correction.

- *Browse button* enables you to scan a list of file names from which you can select a file without typing its name.

- *Check boxes* enable you to select one or more items in a group of options. For example, if you are styling text, you can select both Bold and Italic. Check boxes appear with an "X" or a check mark when selected. Click on a check box to activate it.

- *Option buttons* are like check boxes, but you can select only one option button in a group. Selecting one button deselects any option that is already selected. Click on an option button to activate it.

- *Sample boxes* show you how your selections will affect the document.

- *Command buttons* execute (or cancel) the command once you have made your selections in the dialog box. Some command buttons contain an ellipsis, which indicates that they open additional dialog boxes. To select a command button, click on it.

Switching Between Windows

Many times you will have more than one window open at once. In Organizer, this happens when you open more than one document. To switch among them, do one of these actions:

- Open the Window menu and choose the window you want to view.

- If a portion of the desired window is visible, click on it.

Controlling a Window

As you saw earlier in this appendix, you can minimize, maximize, and restore windows on your screen. But you can also move them and change their size.

- To move a window, drag its title bar to a different location. (Remember, "drag" means to hold down the left mouse button while you move the mouse.)

- To resize a window, position the mouse pointer on the border of the window until you see a double-headed arrow. Then drag the window border to the desired size.

Copying Your Program Diskettes with File Manager

Before you install any new software such as Organizer, you should make a copy of the original diskettes as a safety precaution. Windows' File Manager makes this process easy.

First, start File Manager by double-clicking on the File Manager icon in the Main program group. Then, for each diskette you need to copy, follow these steps:

1. Locate a blank diskette of the same type as the original diskette and label it to match the original. Make sure the diskette you select does not contain any data that you want to keep.

2. Place the original diskette in your diskette drive (A or B).

You Can't Be Too Careful! To make sure that you don't accidentally write over your original program diskette, write-protect it. On a 3 1/2" diskette, slide the little black plastic cover upward to leave the square hole open. To write-protect a 5 1/4" floppy diskette, cover the rectangular notch in the side of the jacket. Either use one of the little patches that came with the disks (usually black or silver), or use something similar, such as a piece of a mailing label.

3. Open the Disk menu and select Copy Disk. The Copy Disk dialog box appears.

4. Select the drive used in step 2 from the Source In list box.

5. Select the same drive from the Destination In list box. (Don't worry; File Manager will tell you to switch diskettes at the appropriate time.)

6. Select OK. The Confirm Copy Disk dialog box appears.

7. Select Yes to continue.

8. When instructed to insert the Source diskette, choose OK since the source (original) diskette is already in the drive. The Copying Disk dialog box appears, and the copy process begins.

9. When instructed to insert the target diskette, remove the original diskette from the drive and insert the blank diskette. Then choose OK to continue. The Copying Disk dialog box disappears when the process is complete.

Repeat these steps for all of the diskettes that came with Organizer. Once you've made copies of the program diskettes, turn to the inside front cover of this book for steps on installing the program.

Glossary

accelerator keys   Keys that you can press to quickly perform a command. These keys are listed on menus next to the command they perform.

Address   A section of Organizer where you record addresses and phone numbers.

Anniversary   A section of Organizer where you can note important dates.

bubble help   A type of help that provides you with fast and easy information about something on the Organizer screen. Bubble help works only with the SmartIcons unless you activate it. To do that, open the Help menu and select Bubble Help. Once bubble help is turned on, simply move the mouse pointer over an object of interest, and then wait until the bubble appears.

Calendar   A section of Organizer where you keep track of important dates.

Calls   A section of Organizer where you track information about calls you need to make or have made, such as their duration and status.

check boxes   Items in a dialog box that allow you to select one or more options in a group of options. For example, if you are styling text, you can select both Bold and Italic. Check boxes appear with an "X" or check mark when selected. Click on a check box to activate it.

click   To move the pointer onto the specified item and press the mouse button once. Unless specified otherwise, use the left mouse button.

Clipboard   An area of memory where information that you cut or copy is temporarily stored.

command button An item in a dialog box that executes (or cancels) the command once you have made your selections in the dialog box. Some command buttons contain ellipses, which indicate that they open additional dialog boxes. To select a command button, click on it.

context-sensitive help A kind of help that, when you ask for it, knows what you're doing and gives you very specific information. For example, if you press F1 while the Save As dialog box is on-screen, you get help on saving files.

Control-menu box When selected, pulls down a menu that offers size and location controls for the window. It's located in the upper left corner of a window.

database A file or a group of related files that are designed to hold information. A database is basically a list, with many columns of information.

dialog box A box that appears on-screen to request additional information when you select a command. You enter the information by using text boxes, list boxes, option buttons, and/or command buttons.

double-click To move the pointer onto the specified item and press and release the mouse button twice quickly.

drag To move the mouse pointer onto the specified item, hold down the mouse button, and move the mouse while holding down the button.

drop-down list An item in a dialog box that is similar to a list box, but only one item in the list is shown. To see the rest of the items, you must open the list. Click on the drop-down list and hold down the mouse button. Drag down the list to select an item, and then release the mouse button.

export Transferring information from its original format into another format. Organizer can export Address records into a file that can be used by dBASE III/IV or any word processor that can read an ASCII text file.

field   A dedicated space in a database record. Specific types of information are stored in specific fields. For example, you store an address in a field used only for that type of information. Each record in a database holds fields that are found in every record.

field mapping   Matching up the fields in an imported database with fields in your Address database. Organizer goes through a similar process when you export information so other applications can accept and utilize it.

floating palette   If the SmartIcon palette is floating, that means it is in its own window rather than being anchored on an edge of the screen. You can move the floating window around on-screen by dragging its title bar, and you can resize the window by dragging its borders.

graphical interface   Computer software that enables you to issue commands to your computer by clicking icons and selecting items from menus rather than typing them in.

icons   Graphic representations of programs. To run a program, you select its icon.

import   Bringing information from one program into another so you can work with it. Organizer can import addresses found in dBASE III/IV, Excel, FoxPro, Lotus 1-2-3, and ASCII text files (such as Windows' Notepad's format).

jump word   In the Help system, these are words that cause more specific Help text to appear when clicked upon. Jump words are usually denoted by the use of green text. Click on a green jump word to learn more about the topic represented by that jump word.

landscape orientation   Printing along the length of a page (as in 11" × 8 1/2").

links   Connections between Organizer sections. Organizer allows you to cross-reference (link) information maintained by some sections of Organizer. You can use these links to quickly jump to a certain Notepad page or to a specific entry in your Address book. An icon appears next to the linked information when you establish a link.

list box   An item in a dialog box that displays available choices. To activate a list, click inside the list box. If the entire list is not visible, use the scroll bar to view the items in the list. To select an item from the list, click on it, or if a text box is provided, type in your selection.

Maximize button   A button that you click to expand a window to fill the screen. When maximized, a window contains a double-arrow Restore button, which returns the window to its original size (when clicked on). The Maximize button is located in the upper right corner of a window.

Minimize button   A button that you click to shrink a window to the size of an icon. It's located in the upper right corner of a window.

modem   A device that enables your computer to communicate with other computers or online services through phone lines. If you have a modem hooked up to your computer, you can use the Dialer program in Organizer to make your calls for you.

mouse pointer   A shape (usually an arrow) on-screen that corresponds to the position of your mouse. You control the pointer by moving the mouse.

network   Two or more computers that are connected in order to share resources (such as a printer) or information.

network administrator   The person responsible for ensuring that the network is running smoothly.

Notepad   A section of Organizer that you can use like a pad of paper.

option buttons   Items in a dialog box that are similar to check boxes except that you can select only one option button in a group. Selecting one button unselects any option that is already selected. Click on an option button to activate it.

page turners Little folded back page corners at the bottom of the Organizer screen that you can click to go back one page, or forward to the next page.

password protection Establishing a code word or password for your data to limit the amount of people who can access it.

Personal Information Manager (PIM) A computer program, such as Lotus Organizer, that helps you quickly access and manage addresses, appointments, task lists, and other personal information.

Planner A section of Organizer that organizes events and related people.

point To move the mouse pointer onto the specified item by moving the mouse. The tip of the mouse pointer must be touching the item.

pop-up menus Organizer offers fast access to common menu commands through pop-up menus. Simply move the mouse pointer over an area you wish to work on, then click with the right mouse button. A pop-up menu appears with commands specific to the object to which you were pointing. Select a command from the pop-up menu by clicking on it.

port A place on your computer where you hook up external devices, such as a modem or a mouse.

portrait orientation Printing along the width (as in 8 1/2" × 11") of the paper.

program group window A window containing program icons that you double-click on to run programs.

pull-down menu bar This bar at the top of an application window contains a list of the pull-down menus available in the program.

record   A group of related fields. In an address database, for example, a record might include a person's name, address, and telephone number.

sample box   An item in a dialog box that shows you how your selections will affect the document.

Schedule Advisor   A component of Organizer that enables you to schedule metings with other people on your network. To use this feature, your network administrator must install Schedule Advisor on your network.

scroll bars   A bar along the side or bottom of a window that enables you to view additional information in the window. *Scroll arrows* on each end of the scroll bar allow you to scroll slowly. The *scroll box* allows you to scroll more quickly.

section tabs   Tabs along the right or left side of the binder (depending on the view). Each of these section tabs represents a section, such as the Address or the Calendar. Click on a tab to switch to that tab's section.

SmartIcon   An icon you can click to run a commonly used task, like opening or saving a file. In Oganizer, SmartIcons are arranged in a horizontal strip near the top of the application window called the *SmartIcon palette*.

text box   An item in a dialog box that allows you to type an entry. To activate a text box, click inside it. To edit an existing entry, use the arrow keys to move the cursor, use the Del or Backspace keys to delete existing characters, and then type your correction.

time tracker   A control that appears when you open the Time drop-down list box in the Create or Edit Appointment dialog box. The time tracker consists of two clocks that show the starting and ending times for the appointment. The duration of the appointment is shown in a small box between the two clocks. You drag the elements of the time tracker either up or down to adjust your appointment.

title bar   A bar at the top of a window that shows the name of the window or program.

To Do list   A section of Organizer where you organize what you need to do and when you need to do it.

Toolbox   An area on the left side of the Organizer window that holds several buttons that let you move entries, link information, turn to the previous page in the current section, send/receive mail, make phone calls, print information, and so on. Simply click the button you want to use.

Trash basket   A place on the Organizer screen that you can drag information you no longer need. When you drag-and-drop text into the Trash, it goes up in "flames."

write-protect   To prevent accidently overwriting data on a diskette by covering the write-protect notch on a diskette or sliding the write protect tab to the appropriate position.

10

Index

PLUG YOURSELF INTO...

The MCP Internet Site

Free information and vast computer resources from the world's leading computer book publisher—online!

Find the books that are right for you!
A complete online catalog, plus sample chapters and tables of contents, give you an in-depth look at *all* our books.

✦ **Stay informed** with the latest computer industry news through discussion groups, an online newsletter, and customized subscription news.

✦ **Get fast answers** to your questions about MCP books and software.

✦ **Visit** our online bookstore for the latest information and editions!

✦ **Communicate** with our expert authors through e-mail and conferences.

✦ **Play** in the BradyGame Room with info, demos, and shareware!

✦ **Download software** from the immense MCP library.

✦ **Discover hot spots** on other parts of the Internet.

✦ **Win books** in ongoing contests and giveaways!

Drop by the new Internet site of Macmillan Computer Publishing!

To plug into MCP:

World Wide Web: http://www.mcp.com/
Gopher: gopher.mcp.com
FTP: ftp.mcp.com

GOING ONLINE DECEMBER 1994